Yeats's
AUTOBIOGRAPHY

Life as Symbolic Pattern

JOSEPH RONSLEY

HARVARD UNIVERSITY PRESS
CAMBRIDGE, MASSACHUSETTS
1968

To Joanne

PREFACE

Although there have been numerous books and articles written during the last several years which cover many aspects of the life and work of William Butler Yeats, and although *The Autobiography* has been put to extensive biographical and critical use during this time, there has never been an extended study of *The Autobiography* in its own right. Since it is one of Yeats's two long prose works, both of which are central in his total oeuvre, there can be no doubt that such a study is called for.

My greatest debt in writing this book is to Professor Richard Ellmann, who more than anyone else gave me the necessary literary training before the book was conceived as well as his guidance during the writing of it, and who generously lent me his copies of Yeats's papers and unpublished writings. I could not have succeeded without him and cannot thank him adequately.

I also wish to thank Professors Glenn O'Malley and Donald Torchiana who read the manuscript in its early stages, making many corrections, and Professor John Unterecker who did so later. Professor Curtis Bradford supplied me with important information regarding Yeats's unpublished writings. Robert Burns and Mrs. Alan Gold of Montreal gave me valuable suggestions in different areas. Richard Olson, curator of rare books at Northwestern University's Deering Library, made my use of early editions of Yeats's works much easier than it might have been.

I am grateful to Northwestern and McGill Universities for providing facilities for research and funds to ease expenses. The Houghton Library, Harvard University, provided a microfilm copy of "Memoirs," Yeats's first draft of *The Trembling of the Veil.*

The Yeats papers and unpublished writings referred to in the text are in the possession of Mrs. W. B. Yeats, Dublin. Senator Michael Butler Yeats and Miss Anne Yeats have kindly given me permission to quote from their father's papers and unpublished writings, © Miss Anne Yeats and Michael Butler Yeats 1968. I am also in debt to Mr. M. B. Yeats and Macmillan & Co. Ltd., London, and The Macmillan Company, New York, for permission to quote from Yeats's works—*The Autobiography, The Variorum Edition of the Poems, A Vision,* and *Essays and Introductions;* to Rupert Hart-Davis and The Macmillan Company for permission to quote from Allan Wade's edition of *The Letters of W. B. Yeats;* and to Appleton-Century, affiliate of Meredith Press, and J. C. and R. G. Medley for permission to quote from George Moore's *Hail and Farewell.* Other quotations are acknowledged specifically in the notes, and I am grateful to have been able to use them.

My wife and my parents, each in their own way, gave me help without which this book could not have been written.

J.R.

Madison, Wisconsin
August 22, 1967

CONTENTS

YEATS'S AUTOBIOGRAPHY

Measurement began our might:
Forms a stark Egyptian thought,
Forms that gentler Phidias wrought.
Michael Angelo left a proof
On the Sistine Chapel roof,
Where but half-awakened Adam
Can disturb globe-trotting Madam
Till her bowels are in heat,
Proof that there's a purpose set
Before the secret working mind:
Profane perfection of mankind.

Under Ben Bulben

one

THE NEED FOR

SELF-PORTRAITURE

Yeats wrote his autobiography in many forms—in poems and plays, in essays which seem objective but are really personal, in *A Vision,* and in *The Autobiography* itself. The following pages treat *The Autobiography* both on its own terms as an individual work of art and in terms of its special function among his other works. I have made no attempt to annotate the book or to correct it for the sake of factual accuracy, but rather to discover the design underlying Yeats's presentation of events, people, and ideas. Where fact is counterposed to Yeats's presentation it is done solely with this object in mind. Such a perspective offers two possible advantages: it illuminates the relation of life to art which was as important a theme as any for Yeats, and it displays the craftsmanship of *The Autobiography,* which must rank as one of the most important works of its kind in English. Yeats's artistic preeminence and his participation in several cultural movements, the complexity of the book's form and the beauty of its style, and the part it plays in Yeats's intellectual framework, all contribute to its importance.

Yeats was candidly eager to blend his life and his art into a single image. As his friend George Russell perceived with some mistrust, "He began about the time of *The Wind Among the Reeds* to do two things consciously, one to create a 'style' in literature, the second to create or rather re-create W. B. Yeats in a style which would harmonize with the literary style."[1] Yeats himself emphasized the importance of this interaction, or blending, in a lecture on contemporary poetry delivered in 1910 when he insisted that the poet's life should be made known in order to bind more closely in the reader's mind his poetry with the living experience: "I have no sympathy with the mid-Victorian thought to which Tennyson gave his support, that a poet's life concerns nobody but himself. A poet is by the very nature of things a man who lives with entire sincerity, or rather the better his poetry the more sincere his life; his life is an experiment in living and those that come after have a right to know it. Above all it is necessary that the lyric poet's life should be known that we should understand that his poetry is no rootless flower but the speech of a man."[2] For Yeats, life and art had to be inseparable, and his determination to fuse them caused him, as Richard Ellmann describes it, "to seek always for patterns and pictures, and to hack and hew at his life until it reached the parabolical meaningfulness he found necessary. He must speak for his generation as well as for himself, and reveal the truth about both."[3] Speaking for his generation and reaffirming the ideas he expressed in 1910, Yeats says in the preface to *The Trembling of the Veil* that his friends "were artists and writers and certain among them men of genius, and the life of a man of genius, because of his greater sincerity, is often an experiment that needs analysis and record."*[4] The

---

artist's life and its expression are mutually inadequate. Only by their being brought together in his symbolic imagination can either life or art have meaning or project truth.

Furthermore, this truth, Yeats said in his last published letter (written January 4, 1939, less than a month before he died), can be known not by abstract thought but only by the embodiment of it in the act of living: "When I try to put all into a phrase I say, 'Man can embody truth but he cannot know it.' I must embody it in the completion of my life. The abstract is not life and everywhere draws out its contradictions. You can refute Hegel but not the Saint or the Song of Sixpence."* [5] Yeats saw *The Autobiography*, in effect a combination of his attempt to live his life with style and to describe that stylized life in the perfected manner of arrière-pensée, as an expression of the truth his life embodied. Although the book is interesting as a biographical, historical, or literary document and obviously may be read to advantage for all these things, he saw it largely in terms of self-characterization informed by philosophy and imagination; its main purpose was to bolster his assertion of the artist's totality by making known his own "experiment in living."

Naturally, its artistic form was always a primary concern. Yeats wrote to his American friend John Quinn on June 5, 1922, that he had finished *The Trembling of the Veil* and had dedicated it to him. He speaks of the historical value of Lady Gregory's memoirs, then in progress, but then says that they are "the reverse of my memoirs in every way, for I could not have quoted a letter or diary without spoiling my effect." [6] His reluctance to intrude factual document into his autobiography because of the danger to the "effect" he was

* Quotations from *The Letters of W. B. Yeats,* edited by Allan Wade, are reprinted with permission of Rupert Hart-Davis and The Macmillan Company. Copyright 1953, 1954 by Anne Butler Yeats.

building there confirms his preoccupation with the artistic, or even dramatic, process rather than with mere chronicle. Again, writing to H. J. C. Grierson in October of the same year, he attributed artistic or at least philosophic unity to *The Trembling of the Veil* by referring to it as "a whole, one part depending upon another and all on its speculative foundation."[7] And to Olivia Shakespear in 1934 he described part of his autobiography as dramatization: "I do nothing all day long but think of the drama I am building up in my *Lady Gregory*. I have drawn Martyn and his house, Lady Gregory and hers, have brought George Moore upon the scene, finished a long analysis of him, which pictures for the first time this preposterous person. . . I am just beginning on Woburn Buildings, building up the scene there. . . It is curious how one's life falls into definite sections—in 1897 a new scene was set, new actors appeared."[8] The alteration of the title to *Dramatis Personae* had the effect of shifting the focus slightly away from Lady Gregory, but also of underlining the conception of his own life as that of a player upon a painted stage.

Stylistic and formal patterns within the book itself are more conclusive than the author's testimony of intention. Although *The Autobiography*'s mosaic of narrative and expository fragments may obscure its unity from the casual reader, this unity does in fact exist, and its variety of literary forms and rhetorical devices evinces more the imaginative artist than the disinterested biographer. Short passages of dialogue animate the narrative throughout the book, and the occasional insertion of verse heightens emotional intensity. The metaphors are often as elaborate as in the poetry, and Yeats has a novelist's eye for scenes of poignant confrontation, at times made more immediate by his sudden shifts from past to present tense.[9] Sudden and dramatic shifts in atmosphere and tone as well help to give *The Autobiography* the kind of variety Yeats valued so highly in Chaucer.

In *Reveries Over Childhood and Youth* and *The Trembling of the Veil* Yeats disguises his research into old letters and diaries in order to evoke a more uncertain, dreamy world out of his own and others' memories made hazy by the passage of many years. In so doing he disarms the criticism of the historian and reserves for himself the freedom to alter history into symbolic patterns out of which he can realize an overall artistic and philosophical design.[10] *Dramatis Personae,* on the other hand, shows a later and different method from the one explained to Quinn, for it is heavily documented with excerpts from letters. And *Estrangement* and *The Death of Synge* are almost verbatim transcriptions of passages from his diary of 1908 and 1909. Notwithstanding their air of improvisation, they occupy a strategic position and combine with *The Bounty of Sweden* to end the book in a way which Yeats evidently intended to be meaningfully conclusive. The effect he sought in the later books was one of actuality, not dream; it was almost polemical. His philosophical design was served by the selection and arrangement of his material.

Parts of *The Autobiography,* then, are built upon an imaginatively subjective patterning of experience, others upon the facts themselves. Yeats's methods changed as he wrote and as the material varied, but in the end both the facts and the subjectively apprehended experience are given, as in the poems, symbolic power. Art, Irish nationalism, and the occult, despite shifts in perspective and mood, provide recurring themes which contribute some sense of unity. The patterning of experience toward unity of being and unity of culture, however, whether imaginary or naturalistic, imbues the work with an overall design that finally justifies Yeats's alteration of the title—in the last edition published before his death— from *Autobiographies* to *The Autobiography.* Yeats conceived that unity of being was a state in which the intellect, joined with the emotions and many seemingly disparate aspects of the individual life and its surroundings, became exalted by fusion. Unity of being is expounded philosophically in *A Vision* and appears in different forms in poems, plays, and essays. In *The Autobiography* it is expressed in terms of Yeats's life. Within the book's context unity of being does not characterize his life, but is a goal toward which his experience is consistently and consciously directed.

The overall design of *The Autobiography* was not fully formulated when Yeats began *Reveries Over Childhood and Youth.* Strictly speaking, *Reveries,* written entirely in 1914, was not the first part of the autobiography to be written: one passage in *The Trembling of the Veil* had appeared as a two-page essay under the title "Verlaine in 1894" in *The Savoy* for April 1896 and the diary entries which make up the substance of *Estrangement* and *The Death of Synge* had been recorded mostly in 1908 and 1909. Although Yeats did not at the time intend to publish his diary as an autobiography, he did see it, according to a 1909 letter to Florence Farr, as a source of material for essays.[11] Several passages were in fact published in this form. As early as June 1911 a group of four, with an introduction, appeared in the *Manchester Playgoer* under the title "The Folly of Argument," and another appeared as "Synge" in the *English Review* for March 1913.

Curtis Bradford suggests in his book *Yeats at Work* that Yeats may have written his diary with Maud Gonne in mind, that he intended it to be a record of his thoughts when they were apart and a subject for discussion when they were together again. On the other hand, Bradford suggests in the light of a passage from the letter of 1909 to Florence Farr that it may have been something similar intended for her.[12] But the first hypothesis gives Maud Gonne too much spiritual authority and the second is unsubstantiated. In any case, Yeats intended the diary for other purposes as well.

He used it as a manuscript book and record of his literary life, as Bradford goes on to say, and as a record of thoughts and events.[13] But he used it primarily to apprehend his mode of experience. Events raised to their symbolic power were to become the substance of an art that was concrete, personal, and even intimate rather than general and abstract. Yeats had been moving toward this kind of subjectivity in his work for some time: by 1891 he had already published, under the pseudonym "Ganconagh," his autobiographical novel *John Sherman*, and later during the nineties events and friends helped to crystallize his egocentric orientation as part of a comprehensive aesthetic outlook. From about 1896 to 1900[14] he struggled with another autobiographical novel, "The Speckled Bird," "a novel that I could neither write nor cease to write which had *Hodos Chameliontos* for its theme,"[15] but this project was left unfinished. Not until *In the Seven Woods* (1903), however, did his poetry begin to set aside the imprecise and fugitive temptations of fairyland for more tangible experience.

In some respects his predilection for this continuity between life and art began with his father's insistence all through Yeats's childhood, that "some actual man" be palpable behind the "elaboration of beauty" in a poem. This "actual man" had to be projected dramatically rather than subjectively because he said also that "personal utterance was only egotism."[16] The relation of the artist's life to his art was part of their dialogue during the rest of J. B. Yeats's life. "I was delighted with your letter insisting on 'intimacy' as the mark of fine literature," the son once wrote. "The contrary thing to this intimacy, which is another name for experience, life, is I believe 'generalization.' And generalization creates rhetoric, wins immediate popularity, organizes the mass, gives political success, Kipling's poetry, Macaulay's essays and so on. Life is never the same twice and so cannot be generalized."[17]

Although Yeats condemns generalization here, and abstraction elsewhere ("The abstract is not life and everywhere draws out its contradictions"), he finds philosophical pursuit important. Generalization and abstraction in themselves are almost always referred to pejoratively, spoken of even with hatred, but Yeats does not mean to do without them entirely. As he said in the 1925 edition of *A Vision*, "Having the concrete mind of the poet, I am unhappy when I find myself among abstract things, and yet I need them to set my experience in order."[18] While certain broad generalities are valid and useful, however, their validity and usefulness are limited. Yeats was as adamant and as persistent in asserting his doctrine of "the thinking of the body" as were the romantic poets who first did so in opposition to eighteenth-century rationalism. Like Blake and Coleridge, he believed that philosophy constructed upon an exclusively intellectual perception of life cannot have value because it yields only a rational, and hence fragmented, perspective. This incompleteness is characteristic of the empirically based rationalism with which science proposes to understand and control experience. Total understanding can come only from passionate apprehension, which the intellect reinforces. "We taste and feel and see the truth. We do not reason ourselves into it," Yeats said in his diary, discarding the purely rational. In another place he is more comprehensive: "We only believe in those thoughts which have been conceived not in the brain but in the whole body."* [19] The philosophical system that Yeats finally evolved

* Quotations from *Essays and Introductions*, by W. B. Yeats, are reprinted with permission of Mr. M. B. Yeats and Macmillan & Co. Ltd., and of The Macmillan Company. © Mrs. W. B. Yeats 1961.

was intended to combine, as Cleanth Brooks has said, "intellect and emotion as they were combined before the great analytic and abstracting process of modern science broke them apart."[20] The intellect, for all Yeats's seeming disparagement of it, has as essential a role to play as the emotions. Philosophy produced out of the union of intellect with emotion can triumphantly involve the whole personality. This is what Yeats meant when he said, "Man can embody truth but he cannot know it"; the understanding necessary to achieve this embodiment is what he was reaching for in his diary.

In the process he would search his experience to discover life's values: "My work is very near to life itself," he reflected, "but I am always feeling a lack of life's own values behind my thought. They should have been there before the strain began, before it became necessary to let the work create its values. This house [Coole] has enriched my soul out of measure because here life moves without restraint through gracious forms. Here there has been no compelled labour no poverty thwarted impulse."[21] The importance of some kind of blending of "life's own values"—those of his thought, of his work, of the "gracious forms," of the freedom to be impulsive— already occupied his mind, as he suggests in the early pages of *The Trembling of the Veil,* long before he began *The Autobiography,* although he had not yet formulated his notions into the more fully conceived philosophy of unity of being. This philosophy when it did come had to possess an intellectual discipline powerful enough to give order and purpose to life while at the same time incorporating spontaneity, ebullience, even wildness; it had to be at once "logical and boundless."

Meanwhile, because philosophy could not be intellectually forced into existence, he could only struggle against generalization and abstraction in his art, striving to make that art concrete and to bring it close to his experience, which itself he had first to understand. During the summer of 1910, for example, he was involved in a quarrel between Lady Gregory and Edmund Gosse. Unhappy with his own involvement, he wrote in his diary on August 8: "Why do I write all this? I suppose that I may learn at last to keep to my own in every situation in life. To discover and create in myself as I grow old that thing which is to life what style is to letters, moral radiance, a personal quality of universal meaning in action and in thought." Whether Yeats ever satisfied himself as to achieving "moral radiance" is uncertain, but he does join intellect with his experience in order to provide "a personal quality of universal meaning": philosophy was to be generated out of the life of the individual. He continues in his diary, discovering universal truths by looking into his own experience:

> I can see now how I lost myself. "I have been trying to recreate in myself the passions" I wrote or some such words. Yes but for me they must flow from reason itself. My talent would fade if I trafficked in general standards and yet Punchinello too is ancient. They dug up a statue of him among the ruins of Rome.
>
> Is not all life the struggle of experience naked, unarmed, timid but immortal against generalized thought, only that personal history in this is the reverse of the world's history. We see all arts and societies passing from experience and generalization and end with experience, that is to say not what we call its "results," which are generalizations, but with its presence, its energy. All good art is experience, all popular bad art generalization.

The conclusion is simplistic, but he is here using his diary to probe and sort out experiences and thereby to "discover and create" value and meaning. In trying to understand what underlay his role in the quarrel, for instance, he found that his passion paradoxically had its origin in reason. By detaching himself from his experience intellectually, through writing, he could apprehend that experience objectively without sacrificing its errant, divergent quality (as he could later imaginatively apprehend the world of becoming by stepping outside it in the form of a golden bird in Byzantium).

Besides gaining an objective look at his experience, he could see himself more clearly as the world saw him—in other words, the projection of his acting self in the diary gave him an objective look at his own personal image. The entry quoted above is followed, accordingly, by the poem later entitled "The Mask," which affirms the power in the world of theatricality, or the willful playing of a part. This power gives rise to the fact that it is not generalization, but the artist's individual experience that underlies the work of art, and in the individual experience the face one presents to the world often plays a greater part than either the more instinctive self behind it or the external world's expectations of behavior.

Yeats's experiences would become more useful to him in his art, then, in proportion to his degree of comprehension of them. Likewise, the palpability of the man behind the poem would increase as his personal image became clearer in his own eyes. Like philosophy, "Art bids us touch and taste and hear and see the world, and shrinks from what Blake calls mathematical form, from every abstract thing, from all that is of the brain only, from all that is not a fountain jetting from the entire hopes, memories, and sensations of the body."[22] And if understanding individual experiences is helpful, putting these experiences together to see what larger patterns of thought and feeling they form would be even more helpful. To do so would not be generalization, but rather a method of achieving keener insight into the meaningful patterns taking form in the course of his life.

Yeats kept his diary during the years 1908 to 1913, the six years immediately preceding his work on *Reveries*. He was intent upon clarifying his personal image and giving his experience concreteness and form, upon putting all into shape for use in his poetry. As had his father, Yeats asserted the importance of the artist's living presence in his art: he writes in 1908, "I find myself at moments desiring a more modern, a more aggressive art—an art of my own day. I am not happy in this mood unless I can see precisely how each poem or play goes to build up an image of myself, of my likes and dislikes, as a man alive today."[23] And in 1913 he writes, "Of recent years instead of 'vision' . . . I have tried for more self portraiture. I have tried to make my work convincing with a speech so natural and dramatic that the hearer would feel the presence of a man thinking and feeling."[24] The man whose presence was being evoked had to be clear in the poet's mind first.

But the personal image emerging from his diary was not to be sufficient in itself. Self-portraiture must be the reflection of a personality more comprehensive than that made manifest simply in the expression of personal experience. About the time he began his diary, Yeats awakened to an interest in his family history, not merely because of a personal interest in genealogy, but because he was convinced, like Vico a century and a half earlier and like his own contemporary, Jung, that the personality he explored in his diary was the cultural as well as physiognomic coalescence of his ancestors. A knowledge of his ancestral heritage would help him to understand more fully his own personality.

By 1909 he and his sister Lily were actively investigating their forebears. In March, while searching for his coat of arms to be used as a book plate, he discovered a Mary Yeats of Lifford who had died in 1673 and wondered if his sister, who had made out the family tree, could trace their family back to her. Yeats had from childhood been fascinated by the sense of the past that surrounded the estates of aristocratic families in the neighborhood of Sligo. Lissadell, home of the Gore-Booths which could be seen from across the bay at Rosses Point, was an especial source of romantic images in his imagination, and it had been as he recognized later a preposterously important day for him when in 1894 he was welcomed into the society of that house. His genealogical investigations now gave his interest a more clearly defined direction, and even more important than Lissadell (though his esteem for this house was abiding) was Lady Gregory's estate, Coole, where he had been spending his summers since 1897. At Coole he was always impressed by the graciousness, taste, and wisdom he believed were made possible through leisure and old traditions, and he wanted to see his own heritage within a similar context. As a child he had been unimpressed by his great-aunt Micky's tales of his flamboyant ancestors, but his newly acquired pride in his family history and especially in those people and events that tied his personal history to the history and character of Ireland is prominent in the early pages of *Reveries*, where his ancestors assume a formative part in the delineation of his personality, and in the 1914 prologue to *Responsibilities*, where he apologizes for having produced only a book to prove his worthiness of their blood.

Yeats's growing preoccupation with self-portraiture was further stimulated by the publication of autobiographies by two people who were once his intimate friends. Both dealt with events in which Yeats had a comparable interest, and, more important, both attempted extensive characterizations of him. One of these friends was Katharine Tynan, toward whom Yeats had even felt at odd moments during the 1880's a kind of boyish love. But although he could write her affectionately and often from London, he says in his unpublished "Memoirs" of 1916-1917 that when in her presence he felt less interest. She is mentioned only once, and then passingly, in his autobiography, though hers—entitled *Twenty-Five Years: Reminiscences*—includes long passages about him.

These passages, while not always evoking the kind of image Yeats might have wished, were not really offensive, and he was even pleased with her conjuring events out of the past. He was distinctly displeased, however, with other things. He wrote to her on December 12, 1913:

> I liked your book very much and not merely because it brought back so many memories. You have the gift to describe many people with sympathy and even with admiration, and yet to leave them their distinct characters . . . I was especially interested in all that period before I knew you. You called up the romance of a forgotten phase of politics and gave it dignity . . . I have often felt that the influence of our movement on the generation immediately following us will very largely depend upon the way in which the personal history is written. It has always been so in Ireland.
>
> I am glad, too, that George Moore's disfiguring glass will not be the only glass.[25]

Yeats was sincere but had reservations, most of which he graciously forbore to mention but at which he might have been hinting when he spoke of his preference for that part of the book dealing with the time before he knew her. He could scarcely have been really enthusiastic, for instance, about her indiscriminate praise of many mediocre people, or about her loose style filled with redundancies and clichés, and he was somewhat piqued by her publication without his permission of several passages from his letters, as he indicates in another part of the letter: "You were not very indiscreet," he says, "though you were a little." He was more disturbed, as he indicates in a letter to Lady Gregory, because the personality evoked by those letters, written when he was a very young man, seemed strange to him.[26] Most disturbing of all must have been Miss Tynan's portrayal of him as a dreamy young genius totally absorbed in poetry and romantically oblivious of the daily happenings and relatively mundane feelings of people around him. His own image in *Reveries* is not entirely inconsistent with this; there are, in fact, occasional passages which suggest that Katharine Tynan may have been at least partially right—when, for instance, he describes himself walking "indifferently through clean and muddy places."[27] But this was an image he was for the most part to go out of his way to shatter by replacing it with one which pictured the merging of an aggressive, worldly personality with the spiritually receptive one inherent in his nature. Perhaps, too, Yeats felt that Katharine Tynan's glass, though not disfiguring like Moore's, was sentimental.

Ave, the first volume of George Moore's *Hail and Farewell,* appeared in 1911, two years before Katharine Tynan's autobiography, and was without doubt the more offensive of the two. But a letter to Lady Gregory just after the book's publication suggests that Yeats was still only vaguely disturbed by what he saw as a distorted image of himself and his national literary movement, and that his primary reactions were of amusement at Moore's lack of sophistication in selecting material and in understanding people and ideas. He is even pleased by Moore's uncharacteristic honesty, which, he felt, bordered on sincerity:

George Moore's *Hail and Farewell* is out, I got it yesterday and have read a good deal of it. It is not at all malicious. Of course there isn't the smallest recognition of the difference between public and private life, except that the consciousness of sin in the matter may have made him unusually careful. It is the first book for ten years where he has not been petulant. It is curiously honest, very inaccurate and I think, for anyone not in the book itself, rather dull. Of course he has lots of unfavourable things to say about everybody but they are balanced by favourable things too and he treats himself in the same way . . . There are things which would seem undignified and spiteful if taken by themselves, but the total impression is more than usually sincere. He certainly does not see either you or I [sic] as we are seen by a sympathetic friend. It is a slightly humorous, slightly satirical but favourable impression. A stranger's impression . . . The book is important for it is just the sort of book that gets in biography.[28]

For a man intent on self-portraiture and for one whose own external image had assumed philosophical significance a "stranger's impression . . . that gets in biography"—an impression that distorts his image before the world—was certainly disturbing; though, because it appeared unmalicious and even favorable at the time, he tried to accept the provocation to battle graciously.

His tolerance was overcome in 1913 by a new thrust from Moore in the form of an article in the *English Review* which included passages from *Vale,* the forthcoming final volume of *Hail and Farewell.* Yeats now awoke to the offensiveness of the portrait in *Ave*[29] while becoming enraged over the present article's accusation that he had attacked the middle classes to which his own ancestors belonged. He expressed his indignation in his diary in 1913,[30] but he chose not to deal with Moore publicly until after Moore's death twenty years later, when he wrote *Dramatis Personae.* That is, he did not deal with Moore by name, but the epilogue to *Responsibilities* (written almost immediately after Moore's article in the *English Review,* since it was published in the *New Statesman* on February 7, 1914) is known to allude to Moore in its closing lines:

> . . . till all my priceless things
> Are but a post the passing dogs defile.* [31]

Moore's essay also had the immediate effect of prodding Yeats into celebrating his ancestors in both verse and prose. By January 1914 he had written the prologue to *Responsibilities* and had begun *Reveries*. On December 29, 1914, just after the completion of *Reveries*, he wrote to his sister Lily: "I have written it as some sort of an 'apologia' for the Yeats family and to lead up to a selection of our father's letters."[32] In poem and book he takes pride in his family connection with men who had powerful personalities and, often, distinguished lives.

Yeats counted his father's personality with the others. He believed that his father, a sensitive and articulate man ("The most natural among the fine minds that I have known . . .") having hitherto expressed only informally in letters and a few scattered essays his own experience as part of the current resurgence of Irish culture, was an untapped source of national vitality.[33] Yeats had for some time intended to publish a selection of the letters, and had even suggested to his father in a letter of November 21, 1912, that he write his autobiography:

I have a great project, would you like to write your autobiography? . . . I suggest . . . that in your first chapter or chapters you describe old relations and your childhood. You have often told us most interesting things, pictures of old Ireland that should not be lost. Then, you could describe your school life and then weave a chapter round Sandymount . . . You might do a wonderful book. You could say anything about anything, for after all, you yourself would be the theme, there would be no need to be afraid of egotism [a reference, evidently, to J. B. Yeats's criticism of "personal utterance"], for as Oscar Wilde said, that is charming in a book because we can close it whenever we like, and open it again when the mood comes . . . It would tell people about those things that are not old enough to be in the histories or new enough to be in the reader's mind, and these things are always the things that are least known.[34]

The general outline Yeats sets out for his father adumbrates the organization of his own *Reveries,* which he began a little over a year later. The first paragraph of his preface, where he says that "because one can always close a book, my friend need not be bored," appears to have grown out of the advice of Oscar Wilde, which he recalls for his father in the letter.[35]

Yeats's perspective on all this activity—the continuation of his diary, his research into the family's heritage, the publication of autobiographies by compatriots, his plans to publish his father's letters and memoirs, and the beginning of his own autobiography—was not confined to a private interest. Seeing himself as the product of a heritage linked intimately with Ireland's history and culture, he also saw his personal history blended with that of his country, and he began to think of his own image as a kind of symbol of Ireland. It was as much with a sense of national feeling as of personal interest that he viewed his work and the work of other Irish artists. He asserted this in a letter to Lady Gregory on November 25, 1914, while *Reveries* was in progress: "I think," he writes, "we shall live as a generation as the Young Irelanders did. We shall not be detached figures. I think it is partly with that motive I am trying for instance to improve my sisters' embroidery and publish my father's letters. Your biography when it comes will complete the image."[36] If the lasting power of the nationalist movement lay in the projection of an image of the generation as a whole, the movement's full significance could be known only through the lives and work of its individual members; to bypass personal history in the approach to a composite image would be to generalize, to become abstract. Writing to John Quinn on June 5, 1922, he said: "I have always been convinced that memoirs were of great importance to our movement here. When I was 20 years old we all read Gavan Duffy's *Young Ireland,* and then read the Young Ireland poets it had introduced to us. Hyde, Russell,

Lady Gregory, my father, myself, will all be vivid to young Irish students a generation hence because of the memoirs we are writing now."[37] Yeats had seen his own work largely in the light of this far reaching perspective for quite a long time, and there can be little doubt that it was powerfully present in his mind when he began his autobiography.

Formulating a total image of himself would help him to imbue his work with "the presence of a man thinking and feeling," but this image could not be isolated; it had become part of a great historical process and of the world he thought and acted in. To see it clearly he had to look into his past and at the people around him who had helped to shape his personality. The personal image thus defined would become, he was convinced, in some measure an image of Ireland itself. By applying the power of his symbolic imagination, he would in the course of writing his autobiography give his life philosophical significance as profanely created reality.

two

PUBLISHING

HISTORY

Yeats began writing *Reveries Over Childhood and Youth* in January 1914 and completed it on Christmas Day of the same year. Although dated 1915, it was published by his sister's Cuala Press on March 20, 1916, by Macmillan, New York, a month later, and by Macmillan, London, the following October.[1] As it happened, another autobiographical work, more fictional in kind, came to his attention precisely during the time he was writing *Reveries*. James Joyce's *A Portrait of the Artist as a Young Man* was serialized in *The Egoist* in twenty-five installments from February 1914 to September 1915. Yeats read the book because he was living at the time with Ezra Pound who had arranged for the serialization, and because Joyce's talent had fascinated him for the past twelve years. In a letter of July 29, 1915, Yeats recommended Joyce to the secretary of the Royal Literary Fund, saying that he had "read in a paper called *The Egoist* certain chapters of a new novel, a disguised autobiography, which increases my conviction that he is the most remarkable new talent in Ireland to-day."[2] While Joyce cannot be considered a shaping force upon his much older compatriot, there is a subtle likeness in the disjointed manner of conjuring up the past with which both writers begin their works. John Synge, too, employed a similar manner in his autobiographical notes.[3] Yeats was definitely familiar with these since Synge had left his unpublished writings in Yeats's charge upon his death in 1909. It is not improbable that both Joyce and Synge awakened Yeats to the possibilities of disconnected narrative as a means of presenting his early life in a manner which was at once personal, realistic, and, in Joyce's case at least, anticipatory of later development. Yeats's images, like Joyce's, come more sharply into focus and acquire a larger measure of continuity as they center on a mind maturing into greater coherence.

Upon completing *Reveries*, Yeats had already decided to extend his autobiography, though he had not yet devised a formal plan for doing so. He wrote to his father on December 26, 1914: "Yesterday I finished my memoirs; I have brought them down to our return to London in 1886 or 1887. After that there would be too many living people to consider and they would have besides to be written in a different way. While I was immature I was a different person and I can stand apart and judge. Later on, I should always, I feel, write of other people. I dare say I shall return to the subject but only in fragments." He was ready to continue his memoir writing a year later, and perhaps had already begun, but he was determined that the material which now occupied him be kept private: "I am going on with the book," he wrote to his father toward the end of 1915, "but the rest shall be for my own eye alone."[4] This work was accordingly never published as a unit, though much of it was incorporated into *The Trembling of the Veil* and a little into *Dramatis Personae*. The manuscript was put away in an envelope labeled: "Private. A First Rough Draft of Memoirs made in 1916-17 and containing much that is not for publication now if ever. Memoirs come down to 1896 or thereabouts. W.B.Y., March, 1921." Bradford shows that the manuscript was in fact begun in 1915, but less convincingly supposes that it was completed before the beginning of 1917. He bases this terminal date on the fact that certain material in "Memoirs" appeared in a more finished form in *Per Amica Silentia Lunae*.[5] It is not necessary to presume that all of "Memoirs" was written earlier than *Per Amica*, however, and the "Anima Mundi" section of the latter is dated as late as May 9, 1917.

The "Memoirs" of 1916-1917 served, like the earlier diary, to objectify Yeats's experience, making it available for poetic use. "I will lay many ghosts," he wrote to John Quinn on August 1, 1916, "or rather I will purify my own imagination by setting the past in order."[6] As Bradford points out, the generally chronological organization of "Memoirs" is much less complex than that of *The Trembling of the Veil*, its rhetoric is less elaborate, and its speculation less abstruse. The influence of *A Vision*, begun between the composition of "Memoirs" and *The Trembling of the Veil*, contributed substantially to the difference, but then the fact that "Memoirs" is a "first rough draft" and not a finished work must also partly account for it. What did not find its way from "Memoirs" into *The Autobiography* was omitted for several reasons. Some of the material dealt too openly with people still living or with those whose memory Yeats did not wish to offend. Hence, he does not repeat certain anecdotes in which Charles Hubert Oldham appears silly in his misguided notions of morality and patriotism, or speak of the syphilis that brought tragedy to Henley's later life. Other material had little relevance or was disproportionately emphasized for the design now crystallizing in Yeats's mind. The proportion of space devoted to occult activities, for example, was reduced by about a third to provide better balance against his other interests, and, for a similar reason, many details of his nationalist activities were obscured in a more general account of his part in the movement.

Still other material was suppressed because it was too personal. Yeats's sexual awakening and his love affairs occupy many pages in "Memoirs," but in *The Autobiography* he made the same kind of omission as that for which Henry Adams has sometimes been criticized in *The Education*. Yeats's brief courtship of the woman he was to marry did not come within the time covered by *The Autobiography*, but he had two love affairs which did—one with Maud Gonne, unrequited at the time, and the other with Mrs. Olivia Shakespear—and each is taken up in some detail in "Memoirs."

The affair with Olivia Shakespear (whom he called Diana Vernon in "Memoirs"), although lasting only about a year, was one of deep feeling and afterwards passed into a nostalgic friendship. Writing to her in 1926 he said that he looked back to his "youth as to [a] cup that mad man dying of thirst left half tasted," and again in 1933, "Yet do I write to you as to my own past."[7] In 1934, writing of his work on what was to become *Dramatis Personae,* he said sadly that "the most significant image of those years [hers] must be left out."[8] The turbulent love affair with Maud Gonne lasted, in some form, right down to the time he put aside his memoirs in 1917 (although it is likely that his last proposal of marriage had been made with the hope and expectation of refusal). His alternately hopeful and frustrating love affair with her is one of the dominant themes in "Memoirs," recurring from her first appearance, which Yeats designates as the time "when the troubles of my life began," until the manuscript ends with his giving her up, saying, "I am too exhausted and can do no more."

His marriage and a concern for the feelings and reputations of the persons involved caused him to omit all reference to

Olivia Shakespear in his published autobiography (he comments even in "Memoirs" that certain incidents must be omitted lest "Diana Vernon's" identity become known) and to avoid dwelling on his feeling for Maud Gonne. In the latter instance he summons up the effect of Maud Gonne's beauty upon him when she first arrived in Bedford Park, then skips to her nationalist activities, which he compares and contrasts with his own. She stays in the background as one of his "Presences," sporadically appearing to him like Venus to Aeneas. But even though he is for the most part reticent, he does recall the attempt he made to persuade her that their efforts to impose national unity upon a discordant Irish society might be more effective if they were to marry each other.

During the few years subsequent to Yeats's memoir writing he was taken up with a variety of activities and interests. After his affair with Maud Gonne ended, he married Georgie Hyde-Lees. They had a child, Anne, sixteen months later. They ordered a local builder to restore Thoor Ballylee, the Norman tower near Gort which Yeats had purchased a few years earlier; the family moved into it in 1919. These years were extraordinarily productive of poetic composition: several poems in the 1919 volume, *The Wild Swans at Coole,* and nearly all in *Michael Robartes and the Dancer* of 1921 were written between 1917 and 1920; *The Only Jealousy of Emer* was written in 1919. Undoubtedly the most important single event of these years in so far as *The Autobiography* is concerned, was the evolution of much of *A Vision* from the automatic writing of Mrs. Yeats. As will become clear, its effect upon the ultimate direction of *The Trembling of the Veil* was determinating. Finally, Yeats made a lecture tour of the United States which lasted into May 1920, and it was probably when he returned to Ireland, fresh from the change of perspective induced by lecturing on the Irish movement in another country, that he resumed work on his autobiography.

Moreover, as he acquired new experience he felt the need for further objectification of his past in order to understand the present. The artistic shaping of his earlier life was an aid to the poems in which he expressed his contemporary experience.

"Four Years: 1887-1891," the first part of *The Trembling of the Veil,* was published in abridged form in three installments—June, July, and August 1921—simultaneously in the *London Mercury* and *The Dial.* It was published complete by the Cuala Press in December 1921.[9] "This memoir writing," Yeats wrote the following year to Olivia Shakespear, "makes me feel clean, as if I had bathed and put on clean linen. It rids me of something and I shall return to poetry with a renewed simplicity."[10] Sending her a copy of the Cuala Press edition, he again wrote to her: "I send *Four Years* which is the first third of the complete memoirs. As they go on they will grow less personal, or at least less adequate as personal representation, for the most vehement part of youth must be left out, the only part that one well remembers and lives over again in memory when one is in old age, the paramount part. I think this will give all the more sense of inadequateness from the fact that I study every man I meet at some moment of crisis—I alone have no crisis."[11] "Four Years" does, in fact, examine each of several friends "at some moment of crisis." Yeats's own crisis had almost brought him to total disillusionment and nervous breakdown during the nineties, when he had given priority to otherworldly experience in an effort to avoid the distressful worldly present. His crisis develops gradually throughout the course of *The Trembling of the Veil,* and is in part implied in the study of the crises of others and of the age itself. It was overcome when he discovered a philosophy by which he could order his life and thereby move with greater assurance toward unity of being.

The periodical publication of "Four Years" met with immediate success. Yeats felt encouraged and wrote Lady Gregory in June 1921 that he would probably continue his autobiography down to the beginning of the Irish Literary Theatre.[12] He was further gratified when T. Werner Laurie, publisher of several limited editions of George Moore's books, offered him £500 for the right to issue "Four Years," although plans had already been made for publication by the Cuala Press. Laurie evidently had made his original offer after seeing the first of the *Mercury* installments, and in 1922 he and Yeats agreed on the terms for publication of the entire *Trembling of the Veil*.

Happy with the success of the periodical publication, Yeats advised George Russell to write his new book in the way he himself was writing his memoirs: he should publish parts of it first in periodicals in order to lighten the larger task. He goes on to describe his plans for the completed work:

I may call the book *The Trembling of the Veil* (Mallarmé said "The whole age is full of the trembling of the veil of the temple") but some better title may occur. You may perhaps have seen what the *London Mercury* has published. I shall insert fresh chapters in that and lead up to the later part and my object will be to suggest, indirectly, things descriptive of characters and events in the main, and only here and there to directly state certain simple philosophical ideas about Ireland, and about human nature in general.[13]

Whether or not the overt "philosophical ideas about Ireland, and about human nature in general" are really "simple" is questionable; that they, along with those things covertly suggested, are complex might be asserted in light of the symbolic autobiographical patterns that ultimately evolved out of the system of *A Vision*.

Bradford establishes that all *The Trembling of the Veil* subsequent to "Four Years" was conceived and written as a unit and that the individual books were marked out late in composition. Before being published in its entirety, further periodical publications were excerpted from it. A series entitled "More Memories," comprising all of "Ireland After Parnell" and parts of "Hodos Chameliontos" and "The Tragic Generation," appeared in the *London Mercury*, May to August 1922, and in *The Dial*, May to October 1922. At this time also, "Four Years" was revised: Yeats added the sections on Florence Farr and Maud Gonne, revised those on Madame Blavatsky and MacGregor Mathers, adding much new material to the latter, and rewrote the conclusion, thereby facilitating a transition to "Ireland After Parnell." *The Trembling of the Veil* was published by T. Werner Laurie in October 1922.[14] There were one thousand copies printed on handmade paper, signed, and issued to subscribers.

In 1923 Yeats received the Nobel Prize for Literature. Though the committee was willing to send medal and money to Dublin, he chose to attend the ceremony in Stockholm. The decision is not surprising in view of the fact that the Norwegian and Swedish drama had helped to inspire his own ambitions for the Irish theater over twenty years earlier. "We have to write or find plays that will make the theatre a place of intellectual excitement," he had written in *Samhain: 1903*, "a place where the mind goes to be liberated as it was liberated by the theatres of Greece and England and France at certain great moments of their history, and as it is liberated in Scandinavia to-day."[15] Accordingly, "The Irish Theatre" was the subject on which he spoke to the Swedish Royal Academy. Almost immediately upon his return to Ireland he began to write out his Stockholm impressions as, he wrote to Lady Gregory, "a sort of 'bread and butter letter' to Sweden, and at last a part of my autobiography."[16] *The Bounty of Sweden*, finished late in January 1924, eventually became the final section of the completed *Autobiography*, but was originally published as an individual book by the Cuala Press in July 1925.

In August of the following year the Cuala Press published *Estrangement: Being Some Fifty Thoughts from a Diary by William Butler Yeats in the Year Nineteen Hundred and Nine.* Yeats had gathered these passages from his 1909 diary, at least partly, perhaps, to keep his sister's press busy, although he may even then have planned to include them in his autobiography in a more coherent form. The work also appeared as *Estrangement: Thoughts from a Diary Kept in 1909* in October and November of that year in the *London Mercury* and in November in *The Dial.* Here, and in *The Death of Synge,* the passages transcribed from the diary were taken essentially intact, though there were several changes which Bradford describes in some detail.[17] Names of individuals were left out or added, passages reflecting disapproval of the Catholic Church and Yeats's "growing conservatism and generally antidemocratic bias" were either softened or removed, and style was improved. Much of the original diary was omitted, Yeats explained, for personal reasons or because the events were too trivial to be included.

Bradford asserts that most of these changes cause both *Estrangement* and *The Death of Synge* to suffer as a living record of these years in Yeats's life: "In both, life has lost most of its accident." But in *The Autobiography* Yeats had no desire to keep the original blurred density of experience. The poet, he said toward the end of his life, "is never the bundle of accident and incoherence that sits down to breakfast; he has been reborn as an idea, something intended, complete. A novelist might describe his accidence, his incoherence, he must not; he is more type than man, more passion than type."[18] Yeats's design was not to recount his life candidly for the psychological interest or entertainment of the curious, or to provide simple psychological or biographical readings of his poems, but to arrange his life into patterns of experience informed by philosophy and moving toward a preconceived goal. It is quite apparent that some parts of his life that would have contributed to this design were eliminated because they were too intimate, but others resisted inclusion by their irrelevance.

By 1926, then, Yeats had published in *Reveries Over Childhood and Youth* and *The Trembling of the Veil* a fairly consecutive, if selective, account of his life from early childhood until about 1897. The "Memoirs" of 1916-1917 supplied many of the missing details and carried the account somewhat further, but this was for his "eye alone."[19] In addition, he had published the excerpts from his diary of 1909 and the account of his trip to Sweden in 1923.

Setting aside the two later fragments, he now revised *Reveries* and *The Trembling of the Veil,* and Macmillan published them together on November 5, 1926, under the title *Autobiographies.* Revisions were mostly in style, which became more direct and economical of phrase, in small facts, and in the elimination of redundancies between the two parts. These redundancies included passages on Dowden, O'Leary, and Taylor, and on Yeats's literary and national hopes for Ireland; in each instance passages were deleted from *Reveries* because of their fuller treatment in *The Trembling of the Veil.* He also expanded the section on his ancestors, evidently, Bradford suggests, because he had learned more about them since 1914.[20]

Of more significance was the addition of three rather extensive passages to *The Trembling of the Veil.* One of these was Section VI of "Hodos Chameliontos," in which Yeats recalls banishing George Pollexfen's hallucinatory "red dancing figures" by invoking the cabbalistic symbol of water. Another, in Section XVIII of "The Tragic Generation," was an expanded evaluation of MacGregor Mathers's career, including Yeats's belief that he had become lost upon *Hodos Chameliontos.*

The final addition, coming in Section VI of "The Stirring of the Bones," is perhaps the most significant. It is the account of advice Yeats received from "a certain symbolic personality" to "live near water and avoid woods 'because they concentrate the solar ray,' " followed by his vision at Tullira Castle and his subsequent investigations into the meaning of both. The vision of the archer, as Yeats came to understand it, was either a glimpse of "some great event taken place in some world where myth is reality," or of something "in the memory of the race . . . believed thousands of years ago."[21] In either case, it was related to the advice he had received through the star, through the children who also had visions, and through the tree in Fiona Macleod's story (as Yeats explains in the note "The Vision of an Archer").[22] In this way both advice and vision were somehow connected with the woods and lake of Coole Park. The implication is that Yeats's friendship with Lady Gregory and his first visit to Coole had a kind of preternatural sanction. Moreover, his account foreshadows and lends credence to another vision coming shortly afterwards at Coole, which was to be the first of a series of visions revealing, finally, the philosophy that by ordering his thought and feeling would impel him toward unity of being.

The two notes at the end of *The Autobiography,* "The Hermetic Students" and "The Vision of an Archer," were also added to *The Trembling of the Veil* for the 1926 edition, the latter having first appeared in *The Criterion* and *The Dial* in July 1923. All these additions have the effect of giving a preternatural dimension to Yeats's life.

Yeats intended to take up his autobiography immediately where he had left off at the end of *The Trembling of the Veil.* His scruple in keeping to the remote past was now set aside, for he wanted to carry it down nearly to the time of writing, though he still meant to put off publication of certain chapters. He complained to Olivia Shakespear in a letter of December 6, 1926, that his work on *Oedipus* was delaying his "new Autobiography. I had hoped," he said, "to bring you chapters not for present publication and hear similar chapters out of yours. My new Autobiography—1900 to 1926 —may be the final test of my intellect, my last great effort, and I keep putting it off."[23] The final test of Yeats's intellect was to express the truth embodied in his life, and it was with this exalted purpose in mind that he rounded out the design of *The Autobiography.*

It was put off even longer than he anticipated. During the following year, aside from adapting *Oedipus* for the Abbey Theatre, he was absorbed in writing verse, in continuing work on *A Vision,* and in participating in the Irish Senate. In the fall of 1927 he became ill with a lung ailment and moved first to Spain and then to the south of France in search of a more congenial climate. He still planned to continue his autobiography, however. In a letter written to Mrs. Shakespear from Cannes on November 29, 1927, he said that he was going back to work in spite of his illness and that he felt great joy in doing so. George Moore's *Hail and Farewell* was still to be answered, and the next section of his autobiography was to cover that period of his life which included Moore ("I did hate leaving the last word to George Moore," he said in his letter).[24] But other interests again turned him aside, and he was not to complete *Dramatis Personae* until eight years later. But meanwhile, in April 1928 the *London Mercury* and *The Dial* carried "The Death of Synge, and other Passages from an Old Diary." *The Death of Synge* was published by the Cuala Press in June 1928.

It was only after Lady Gregory's death in 1932 that Yeats again took up his autobiography. He was planning to write a reminiscence of Lady Gregory and of Coole, and had even made arrangements with Macmillan for its publication. But *The Trembling of the Veil* ended shortly after his first meeting with her, and any continuation of his autobiography would naturally begin with their friendship. The same material could serve here or in a reminiscence of Lady Gregory, but the shift away from his own interests to hers might prove distracting. On November 11, 1933, he implied in a letter to Mrs. Shakespear that he was anxious to complete his autobiography, and another letter, written February 27, 1934, indicates that he had now expanded his subject considerably beyond Lady Gregory.[25] The idea of a simple memoir had definitely given way. Her name still served as the title, however, and although this was ultimately changed to *Dramatis Personae,* there is no question that she is the center of the book. George Moore, who had died the previous year, also plays a prominent role but chiefly as the antagonist. The book was published on December 9, 1935, by the Cuala Press. It appeared in the *London Mercury* in November and December of that year and in January 1936, and in the *New Republic* in February, March, and April 1936. Lady Gregory had left her unpublished memoirs in Yeats's charge and he had obtained the letters he had written her. Feeling the need to settle issues of fact in this book, he studied the memoirs carefully and quoted freely from the letters.

Dramatis Personae carried Yeats's life from 1896 to 1902. Although he had planned, as he told Mrs. Shakespear, to carry it down to 1926, the poor state of his health at the time and the subsequent publications combining segments of his autobiography which had earlier appeared separately indicate that he considered any immediate further progress unlikely. His health was beginning to fail significantly and he spent most of his time in southern Europe. In May 1936, the Macmillan Company, New York, and Macmillan and Company, London, published *Dramatis Personae,* now comprising, in addition to the title section, *Estrangement, The Death of Synge,* and *The Bounty of Sweden,* arranged according to the chronological order of events. There was little revision from the original publications of these books, though there was some in matters of detail. The preface and several notes included in the 1925 edition of *The Bounty of Sweden* were dropped, thereby tending to subordinate the occasion itself to its part in Yeats's overall design.

On August 30, 1938, the Macmillan Company published all six books in a single volume for the first time as *The Autobiography* of William Butler Yeats. This was the last edition of Yeats's autobiography published during his lifetime; it appeared four months before his death, and twenty-two years after the first publication of *Reveries Over Childhood and Youth*. Although it seems fragmentary and lacks unity of form, Yeats must have seen the book as a unified whole rather than a series of individual pieces, because he changed the title from the original plural form of 1926, when the work actually appeared to be more unified, to the singular. And *The Autobiography* does succeed in focusing, as Yeats intended, upon the pattern evolving out of his struggle for unity in both his own life and in that of his country.

three

EXFOLIATION

Yeats begins *Reveries Over Childhood and Youth* as if he were writing about the beginning of the world. He enumerates sense impressions and random glimpses of his surroundings to produce an image of childhood, and in this way unfolds an Edenic view of his own beginnings. The opening lines elicit a mood of reverie which is intensified with the earliest fragments his memory can recall: he looks out of a window in Ireland at a cracked wall, then out of one in London at the telegraph boy who he fears is going to blow up the town; after this "come memories of Sligo."[1] Memories are made simultaneous by the dissolution through the intervening years of sequential order: "I do not know how old I was (for all these events seem at the same distance) when I was made drunk," and, "At Ballisodare an event happened that brought me back to the superstitions of my childhood. I do not know when it was, for the events of this period have as little sequence as those of childhood."[2] In this apparent discontinuity Yeats is subtly preparing the way for more detailed recollections of each of the places so briefly evoked.

Although nearly all the images evoked by memory are "fragmentary and isolated," they vary in range of clarity and amount of detail. Sometimes they are uncertain, almost speculative: "Perhaps my mother and the other children had been there all the time, for I remember my father now and again going to London."[3] Or the recollection may penetrate deeply enough to resurrect fully a moment of youthful introspection accompanied by a comparably youthful outburst of confidence and ambition:

Two pictures come into my memory. I have climbed to the top of a tree by the edge of the playing field, and am looking at my school-fellows and am as proud of myself as a March cock when it crows to its first sunrise. I am saying to myself, "If when I grow up I am as clever among grown-up men as I am among these boys, I shall be a famous man." I remind myself how they think all the same things and cover the school walls at election times with the opinions their fathers find in the newspapers. I remind myself that I am an artist's son and must take some work as the whole end of life and not think as the others do of becoming well off and living pleasantly.[4]

The fragments often take on psychological patterns: "All the names and faces of my school-fellows have faded from me except one name without a face and the face and name of one friend, mainly no doubt because it was all so long ago, but partly because I only seem to remember things dramatic in themselves or that are somehow associated with unforgettable places." Still others are inspired by specific places or events: "A poignant memory came upon me the other day while I was passing the drinking-fountain near Holland Park, for there I and my sister had spoken together of our longing for Sligo and our hatred of London."[5] Yeats's early life is recalled in isolated fragments, then, and his memories are evoked in different ways and in varying degrees of intensity.

An atmosphere of reverie pervades the book and is the key to its structure. The disjointedness of images, diversity of their recall, and range of clarity combine to display a dream-like view of the world that defies the order in which we are accustomed to experience it. This view elicits a sense of Yeats's past that in its freshness and strangeness becomes primal. Synge in his own autobiographical writing had said, with perhaps a greater Darwinian turn than Yeats would give it: "If by the study of an adult who is before his time we can preconstruct the tendency of life and if—as I believe—we find in childhood perfect traces of the savage, the expression of a personality will reveal evolution from before history to beyond the science of our epoque."[6] Vico and Yeats both say that we duplicate the history of man in each individual consciousness.

Within this framework of disconnected reverie Yeats recalls the history of his own consciousness through the growth of his interests rooted there. Later he apportioned these interests into three motifs—art, Irish nationalism, and philosophy—and ultimately attempted to draw them together until they fused. *The Trembling of the Veil* is concerned with his attempt to resolve the multiplicity into unity. Although it is unlikely that Yeats in 1914 foresaw precisely the function of *Reveries Over Childhood and Youth* within the completed *Autobiography,* this opening section prepares for his resolution by displaying his separate interests as they developed and the exfoliation of his personality.

Yeats begins with an account of his family, drawing for the purpose on his own memory and the memories of others. In chronicling his family history he rebuts George Moore, who had accused him of being ashamed of his middle-class background. Far from being ashamed, he takes pride in the individuality and strength of personality displayed by his relatives both in the past and in his own lifetime, and in whatever actions linked them with Irish history. In describing their quirks and excesses, and a characteristic insouciance, he renders his family proof against the charge of mediocrity. An element of romance pervades all three family branches with which he is concerned, but of the three the Yeats branch was most picturesque, he says, including many men who played a role of one kind or another in the history of Ireland. Some won fame, some notoriety, but nearly all secured some sort of conspicuousness. And while Yeats does not say it outright, he actually implies a distinction in the "stock" of both the Yeatses and his mother's family, the Pollexfens, an aristocracy of temperament if not of birth. In refuting Moore's charge of snobbery, Yeats dissociated his family from bourgeois crassness or philistinism.

Yeats is not boasting in this account of his forebears. He allows that most of them were not aristocrats but merchants, yet also takes pride in many who were of consequence to the state, or had about them the qualities of eccentricity and even heroism that he always admired. The portraits in *Reveries* elaborate on those which celebrate his ancestors in verse:

> Merchant and scholar who have left me blood
> That has not passed through any huckster's loin,
> Soldiers that gave, whatever die was cast.[7]

His childhood days in Sligo where he spent the summers (he recalls almost nothing of Dublin) were dominated by relatives who lived in the neighborhood, but among them his earliest memories center on "the daily spectacle" of his Pollexfen grandparents; *Reveries,* and his youth itself it would seem, end with their deaths. Most poignant of all is the image of his grandfather:

> You most of all, silent and fierce old man,
> Because the daily spectacle that stirred
> My fancy, and set my boyish lips to say,
> "Only the wasteful virtues earn the sun."[8]

The heroic proportions of William Pollexfen in his grandson's memory make him a semi-legendary figure and an abiding influence. Yeats says that the delight in passionate men manifest in his poems and plays might have its origin in the memory of his grandfather, and that he sought out at least one friend, William Morris, because of his resemblance to his "old grandfather in Sligo."[9]

Among the aunts and uncles whom the tradition of eccentricity—especially as connected with occult interests—also had not allowed to fade from his memory, are his uncle Alfred Pollexfen, and another Pollexfen uncle who was a talented man but slightly mad. Still another, George Pollexfen, with whom Yeats came to be on the most intimate terms of all, comes into prominence later in the book. The Middletons, the other branch of his mother's family, like the Pollexfens were merchants, but unlike them they were practical people and relatively bland. Yet from them Yeats may have received his first interest in country stories, and one among them at least, he says, had second sight. As the book proceeds, it becomes clear that one of its major recurring themes centers on personality itself. Yeats found it in colorful abundance among his Sligo relatives. His own personality emerges gradually during the course of *Reveries,* and *The Trembling of the Veil* indicates that in choosing friends later in life, even aside from Morris, his preference for a powerful personality often caused him to set aside intellectual or temperamental incompatibilities.

Yeats inherited his attitudes toward personality in large measure from his father. As both saw it, personality was not merely the individual's complex of distinguishing external characteristics and mannerisms, but was more comprehensively "a bundle or mass of instincts, appetites, longings, psychical intuitions, resting on the firm basis of the five senses."[10] Intellect served only to harmonize these ordinarily anarchic elements into a total personality; emotion was the common denominator among them. J. B. Yeats had written to Edward Dowden in 1869, professing his complete fidelity to the power of the emotions: "In the completely emotional man the least awakening of feeling is a harmony, in which every chord of every feeling vibrates . . . With you intellect is the first thing and the last in education. With us [the "brotherhood" consisting of the artists Nettleship, Wilson, Potter, Page, and himself], with me at any rate, and with everybody who understands the doctrine, emotion is the first thing and the last."[11] He overstates his case, but it was necessary for him, as it had been for Blake, to relegate a reasoning faculty too highly esteemed by most of the world to its proper relationship with the other human faculties. Both father and son, in fact, had a much greater respect for the power of the intellect than this letter suggests, but Yeats takes up his father's metaphor as late as the composition of *A Vision* when he describes the "opening of the tinctures" that begins to make unity of being possible at phases eleven and twelve. The "completely emotional man" is implied at this stage where, he says, "sexual love becomes the most important event in life . . . Personality seeks personality. Every emotion begins to be related to every other as musical notes are related. It is as though we touched a musical string that set other strings vibrating."*[12] Both *A Vision* and *The Trembling of the Veil* make clear, however, the importance of the intellect's harmonizing power in ordering and giving authority to the emotions and thereby in giving depth and wholeness to the personality.

The ambivalence of J. B. Yeats's attitude toward the relation of intellect to emotion was also clear: he was intellec-

* Quotations from *A Vision,* by W. B. Yeats, are reprinted with permission of Mr. M. B. Yeats and Macmillan & Co. Ltd., and of The Macmillan Company. © The Macmillan Company 1961.

tually sceptical and utilitarian in regard to religion, and at
the same time tended in his daily life to minimize the importance of the intellect in favor of emotion. Emotions should
enlarge the mind, not diminish it, he believed, and ideas
should serve the mind, not enslave it. Servile devotion to an
abstract intellectual principle would destroy the human soul
just as effectively as servile religious devotion destroys the
mind. The artist, particularly, must be encouraged to change
his intellectual conviction from day to day so long as he maintains integrity of the soul, that is, so long as he believes sin-
cerely in his conviction of the moment.

J. B. Yeats's views are important here, first, because his
concept of the personality was one which Yeats abided by in
its essentials and which consequently pervades his analyses of
various personalities throughout *The Autobiography,* and
second, because he was the major influence in Yeats's life
during the early events recounted in *Reveries.* Yeats's boy-
hood interest in science was largely the result of his father's
influence, and his early artistic development was completely
dominated by him. Yeats fully recognized the significance of
his father's role and emphasized it. He writes to his father
on December 26, 1914, just after completing *Reveries:* "Some
one to whom I read the book said to me the other day: 'If
Gosse had not taken the title you could call it *Father and
Son.'* "[13] The tone suggests filial harmony, though much of
Reveries is, in fact, concerned with the filial conflict arising
out of Yeats's struggle to find his own identity and to assert
a personality independent from that of his father.

His enthusiasm for science, initially stemming from his father's religious scepticism, quickly began to decline. Soon he
would reject it altogether in favor of more spiritual interests,
and grow to hate science "with a monkish hate."[14] But despite
this hatred, his affirmation of more imaginative, or spiritual,
sources of knowledge was always tempered by at least a quasi-

scientific attitude. His occultism, for example, often differed from that of friends or fellow-occultists in his willingness to investigate by experiment before accepting any dogma as true or phenomenon as real. The close observation of nature also continued, only now with the object, not of satisfying a scientific curiosity, but of acquiring symbols for poetry.[15]

Poetry, of course, was to be the permanent interest, and its development, along with that of Irish nationalism and occultism, occupies the larger part of *Reveries*. The interests themselves developed concurrently, and Yeats's disjointed method of presentation preserves a sense of this, but their individual developmental patterns are more clearly seen when taken up individually.

Yeats's literary interest began under the auspices of the stable boy at his grandfather's house, he tells us, but he was still very young when his father began making him acquainted with the literature he considered appropriate for his age—first Scott, then Chaucer, Balzac, Shakespeare, and the romantics. During his mid-teens his father's influence upon his thoughts "was at its height."[16] Yeats attributes to these years his convictions, later strengthened and made more complex, that art must be rooted in concrete and personal experience rather than in general and abstract principles, and that beauty of speech is an ultimate objective of poetry.[17] The relationship between his father and himself which he describes in *Reveries,* and again in "Memoirs," is suffused with an atmosphere of rebellion, but in the end they shared more beliefs than they quarreled on.

J. B. Yeats not only influenced his son's artistic awakening directly, but he introduced him to other artists who were his friends, always, however, coloring the ensuing relationship with his own opinions. Yet in delineating the personalities of these artists Yeats manages to objectify and evoke his own personality by his responses to them, and at the same time to present in the aggregate of characterizations a comprehensive image of the artist's milieu he was entering.

His original impression of Edward Dowden, the first notable literary figure in his life, was naively enthusiastic; Yeats found in him qualities of graciousness, culture, intelligent sensitivity and sympathy, and even romance. Still more important, Dowden became an instrument of rebellion against his father, since J. B. Yeats did not share his son's enthusiasm. Yeats soon became disillusioned himself, although it was some time before he broke with him completely. Years later he discovered the real nature of his father's friendship with Dowden, including the reasons for their discord: "Living in a free world accustomed to the gay exaggeration of the talk of equals, of men who talk and write to discover truth and not for popular instruction, he had already, when both men were in their twenties, decided it is plain that Dowden was a Provincial."[18] The manner in which Yeats elucidates his father's attitude testifies clearly to his own support of it.[19]

Most of his father's friends were painters rather than writers, though they did tend to be literary painters. Bedford Park was an exciting place for Yeats when his family moved there in 1876, and the family only "knew the most beautiful houses, the houses of artists."[20] Those whom Yeats recalls were all at one time influenced by the Pre-Raphaelite movement, and all only partially successful and beyond the peaks of their careers. His first memories of the conversation of artists were of an idealism and vitality combined with moments which we are made to feel were sad and somewhat discouraging, since these men were older, often morbidly eccentric, and made melancholy by failure and incipient old age, and by the knowledge that they were part of an artistic era then being displaced by a new one. They created about them, nevertheless, an atmosphere where the sensitivity and values of the artist were supreme, and Yeats was greatly stimulated by it.

Upon returning to Dublin he attended art schools himself, and here too his father rather than the masters was his teacher. The masters "understood nothing but neatness and smoothness," and the students admired and rejected indiscriminately what it was the vogue to admire and reject.[21]

It is not surprising, then, that J. B. Yeats's influence over his son's early poetic composition was as powerful as over his painting and the molding of his literary taste. *Reveries* suggests the power of this influence, and the undercurrent of filial rebellion becomes pronounced in this area. Yeats's first recollection of his own poetic composition is that he was writing poetry in imitation of Shelley and Spenser, "play after play—for my father exalted dramatic poetry above all other kinds—and I invented fantastic and incoherent plots."[22] In *Reveries* he recounts one of these plots, one which Ellmann describes as "the worst and most ambitious of the group."[23] The play, called "Love and Death," is built partly on a theme which expresses Yeats's frustration at his father's overbearing influence, but, perhaps to avoid hurting his father's feelings, he altered the plot in retelling it in *Reveries* (where this expression would have become explicit), obscuring all suggestion of filial conflict.

Yeats indicates that he soon began to oppose his father's views with greater self-assurance. He had been moved by the power given to flat and empty verses when spoken with the intensity of feeling that John F. Taylor could give them, and by other mediocre verse if it but seemed to reflect real thoughts and emotions. As a result he became convinced that sincere emotion was the first requirement in literature. He told his father that poetry should express the poet's own thoughts and feelings with as little embellishment as possible. His father disagreed, contending that "personal utterance was only egotism," but Yeats was sure that it was not, and began to force himself to write without ornamentation, to express his feelings purely, without trying to make them more intense

or more beautiful.[24] Later, the inadequacies of his fellow
Rhymers taught him that his confidence in the value of so
all-absorbing a personal expression was excessive. The work
of those poets lacked the ideas necessary to control the natural
anarchy of their emotions, and this, he believed, contributed
to their failures. Lyric poetry, however, with all its intimacy,
became the genre in which his genius was to find its fullest
expression, and his father evidently accommodated himself to
it. But Yeats recalls his own mixed feelings of annoyance and
approval upon first realizing that Dowden had become his
sage largely by force of insincere condescension "to everybody
and everything." He was then about to learn, he says, "that
if a man is to write lyric poetry he must be shaped by nature
and art to some one out of half a dozen traditional poses, and
be lover or saint, sage or sensualist, or mere mocker of all
life; and that none but that stroke of luckless luck can open
before him the accumulated expression of the world. And
this thought before it could be knowledge was an instinct."[25]
Dowden had merely taken on the sage's traditional pose;
Yeats eventually took on all of them. When the instinct did
become knowledge it evolved into his doctrine of the mask
(and in the process avoided the romantic egoism that so annoyed his father), but when he was twenty-one years old his
poetic theory was as inchoate as his verse.

In the earliest stages of literary thought his father encouraged him and helped more than anyone else to mold his
taste and ideas;[26] later he became a kind of antagonist in
his son's struggle for intellectual and artistic independence.
Yeats felt that he and his father were in the same camp, but
in his early life he magnified their differences and throve on
the conflict of the generations.

The great initial break toward independence came through
mystical philosophy. Yeats takes the reader through his first
tentative efforts to conduct spiritual investigations in the

Hermetic Society and elsewhere against his father's opposition,[27] but *Reveries* lays the groundwork for this interest in occultism in his Sligo childhood. As a child he had listened with fascination to servants and local rustics tell stories about the fairies and other supernatural beings. Soon he was experiencing first-hand, as he thought, the fairies' mischief, foreknowledge coming in dreams, and unnatural lights and noises.[28] The account of these rudimentary occult experiences serves to justify his receptivity of a more sophisticated occultism when he was older. His personal response to them, according to *Reveries,* was not so much to seek intellectual confirmation as to accept them emotionally, on faith, thereby allowing them to furnish an object (of which he had been deprived by the scepticism of his father and the scientists) toward which his naturally religious inclination could be directed. Notwithstanding a later assertion that it was many years before his interests in literature and philosophy came together,[29] they were now already brought somewhat into conjunction, since art, as well as the spiritual belief on which his philosophy was to become founded, was also a matter of emotional rather than intellectual acceptance. At the formation of the Hermetic Society he proposed "that whatever the great poets had affirmed in their finest moments was the nearest we could come to an authoritative religion, and that their mythology, their spirits of water and wind were but literal truth."[30] He had not yet formally embarked on his Blake studies, but an interest in Blake, and an even stronger fascination with Shelley made it easy to see legend, mystery, and poetry as all part of the same mental, or spiritual, activity.

The early romantic poets had nearly a century before asserted the power of the emotions to discover truth, and Blake, Coleridge, and Shelley particularly had asserted the power of the imagination to create reality. Yeats had already been convinced by their doctrines, but now the Brahmin philosopher Mohini Chatterjee, speaking to the Hermetic Society shortly after its inception, gave philosophical authority to his conviction. "Consciousness, he taught," Yeats recalls in *Reveries,* "does not merely spread out its surface but has, in vision and in contemplation, another motion and can change in height and in depth."[31] Yeats wrote several poems at this time which reflect the impact of these ideas on him.[32] In "The Indian Upon God," for example, a vertical movement of consciousness is evident in each creature's vision of God as a higher manifestation of itself: an "undying moorfowl," a giant lotus flower, "gentle roebuck," and "a monstrous peacock."[33] In "The Indian to His Love" the lover sees his love transcending himself and his beloved and becoming part of all nature.[34]

Yeats's absorption in Eastern philosophy, which included also his reading of spiritual and occult works such as Renan's *Life of Christ,* and A. P. Sinnett's *Esoteric Buddhism* along with other Theosophical books, abetted a developing occult interest still more esoteric which came to an early traumatic climax with his first seance.[35] Throughout the course of *Reveries,* his interest in occultism, or spiritual philosophy, intensifies as it evolves from a fascination with rustic tales and superstitions, and his own uncanny experiences, to an interest in Eastern philosophy and his active participation in esoteric hermetic experiments.

If Yeats's interest in the occult enabled him to escape somewhat his father's domination, he also found a measure of personal freedom in his pursuit of Irish nationalist activities, but in this his father was not hostile. It was not long, of course, before both interests far transcended his motive of filial independence. His interest in Irish nationalism, as in literature and in the occult, began in childhood, and *Reveries* here too evokes a pattern of developing scope and enthusiasm throughout his youth.

This pattern begins with fond memories of Sligo and an account of the family heritage which provided him with so many links to Irish history. The appreciation of his forebears, he says, did not come until after he had reached adulthood, but features of the landscape and the attitudes of his kinsmen caused the notion of a distinct Irish identity to be embedded in his mind from the beginning. Although his people in Sligo were confirmed Unionists, their pro-British feeling was confined to politics, and Yeats traces his pride in Irish culture back to their otherwise anti-British prejudices (not to their Celtic pride, for they were as anti-Catholic as anti-British) and to those of their servants and neighbors. His sense of alienation from British culture became acute when the family moved to London and he attended the Godolphin School in Hammersmith. At the Godolphin School his nationalist feeling was aroused first when he was persecuted by the other boys for being Irish, and again when, even after having been accepted by them, he could not share their cultural and historical anecdotes and images, which he maintains are the bases of national identity.

But it was John O'Leary who was ultimately to have the most lasting influence upon his national and political outlook. Yeats was introduced to him at the Dublin Contemporary Club, a discussion group founded and presided over by Charles Hubert Oldham of Trinity College, also founder of the ambitious but short-lived *Dublin University Review* in which many of Yeats's earliest poems were first published. Yeats had begun to frequent the club, he says, for the opportunity of speaking in public and engaging in direct argument with "hostile minds"; he wanted to overcome his natural timidity among strangers and generally to gain self-possession. All subjects were discussed at the Contemporary Club, but politics most frequently; all points of view were represented, but nationalist sentiment prevailed. Here, in spite of his coming out of quite different motives, Yeats's interest in the Irish national movement first became serious under the spell of John O'Leary's personality and idealism.

Yeats attributes the power of O'Leary's influence not so much to his politics as to his romantic past, his heroic mien, the moral force which informed everything he did, and his spontaneous utterance of powerfully emotional sentences. These traits and manners gave him a strength of personality which is thrown into still greater relief by being contrasted to the character of John F. Taylor, who "except at moments of public oratory"[36] lacked entirely the personality so revered in *Reveries*. When he was with O'Leary, Yeats felt like the artist in the presence of his theme.

O'Leary's nationalist vision was dominated by relatively non-political attitudes embracing an outlook more comprehensive than that which mere practical politics could give. Yeats recalls in *Reveries* that O'Leary introduced him to the writings of the Young Irelanders who had initiated his own conversion to the nationalist movement. In the 1915 edition he also recalls other books brought to his attention by O'Leary, which were part of the typical Irish Catholic's heritage; they included Irish geography, history, and poetry, and O'Leary added of his own accord folklore, English history, and the classics as things "Irishmen should know."[37] It was O'Leary's transcendent approach, along with his powerful personality and spacious vision, that set the tune for Yeats's own variety of nationalism and that had a great deal to do with the original awakening of his enthusiasm.

The nationalist spirit always captured Yeats's imagination more than did the political principle, and this can be seen clearly both in his autobiography and in his poems that deal with the subject. He associated the spirit with universal human values and emotions, and made it into their symbol, but the political principle could be no more than a passing and

provincial interest. "The fascination of the national movement for me in my youth," Yeats wrote in his diary, "was I
think that it seemed to be an image of a social ideal which
could give fine life and fine art authority." Out of this fascination grew his longing for a cultural unity to be achieved
by combining an enlightened nationalism and literature: "I
thought we might bring the halves [Catholic natural emotion, and Protestant taste and breeding] together if we had
a national literature that made Ireland beautiful in the
memory, and yet had been freed from provincialism by an
exacting criticism, an European pose."[38] There is a suggestion
of disappointment, of unrequited dream, in this statement
which is elaborated upon more fully in the 1915 edition of
Reveries:

I saw that our people did not read, but that they listened pa-
tiently . . . and saw that there must be a theatre, and if I could
find the right musicians, words set to music. I foresaw a great deal
that we are doing now, though never the appetite of our new
middle-class for "realism," nor the greatness of the opposition, nor
the slowness of the victory. Davis had done so much in the four
years of his working life, I had thought all needful pamphleteering
and speech-making could be run through at the day's end, not knowing that taste is so much more deeply rooted than opinion that
even if one had school and newspaper to help, one could scarcely
stir it under two generations. Then too, bred up in a studio where
all things are discussed and where I had even been told that in-
discretion and energy are inseparable, I knew nothing of the conservatism or of the suspicions of piety. I had planned a drama like
that of Greece, and romances that were, it may be, half Hugo and
half de la Motte Fouqué, to bring into the town the memories
and visions of the country and to spread everywhere the history and
legends of mediaeval Ireland and to fill Ireland once more with
sacred places. I even planned out, and in some detail, (for those
mysterious lights and voices were never long forgotten,) another
Samothrace, a new Eleusis. I believed, so great was my faith, or so
deceptive the precedent of Young Ireland, that I should find men
of genius everywhere. I had not the conviction as it may seem, that

a people can be compelled to write what one pleases, for that could but end in rhetoric or in some educational movement but believed I had divined the soul of the people and had set my shoes upon a road that would be crowded presently.[39]

These feelings become in large part the subject matter of "Ireland After Parnell" in the 1926 edition of *Autobiographies*. Yeats put off the account of his disillusionment so that *Reveries* could focus more sharply on his waxing nationalist enthusiasm.

Reveries, then, chronicles the origins and development of Yeats's three most important lifelong interests. But while his reverie centers much of the time upon the external forces that influenced the development of his interests, these forces are ultimately important only in so far as they bear on the unfolding of his personality, whether they do this by transmitting his cultural heritage, by giving him models on which he could measure his own traits, or by stimulating a multiplicity of interests. During the course of the book his reverie also evokes rather directly, and with considerable clarity, his emerging personality itself.

Yeats portrays himself as a timid, unhappy child, physically delicate and given to extensive daydreaming, but he delineates at the same time with increasing forcefulness a counter-movement toward an independence of spirit and power of self-assertion. He had described the hero of his unfinished autobiographical novel as having been like the "speckled bird" who has "all the birds of heaven . . . against it" and who wonders "why the other birds are so angry."[40] But most of his childhood pain, according to *Reveries,* had its source in his imagination; his fondest memories are of Sligo, memories which made London hateful for him in his youth. "Nobody," he says, "was unkind,"[41] and although he lacked childhood companionship, he had many favorite secret retreats of the kind that children take pleasure in, and was treated to an abundance of the exotic tales that appealed to his youthful romantic temperament. There was plenty of leisure in which to dream of future glory, and companionship did come by way of animals. He had a pony, and the two dogs he describes in *Reveries* were, he wrote to Katharine Tynan, a further stimulus for his dreams.[42] He delighted in fairy tales and later his imagination was stirred by romantic notions of the Godolphin School because its founder had appeared in a novel.

It was the apparent idleness that accompanied his dreaming that his father set out zealously to curb, but his romanticism lasted well into adulthood. Yeats himself did not look upon it as idleness. In an early poem, "The Song of the Happy Shepherd," he is nostalgic about the dreamy days he recalls in *Reveries:*

> The woods of Arcady are dead,
> And over is their antique joy;
> Of old the world on dreaming fed;
> Grey Truth is now her painted toy.

Grown older, he finds dreams no longer adequate, but he echoes the nostalgia of the opening lines in lamenting a lost dreamy youth, for those dreams had value not obtainable in the "Grey Truth" of adulthood:

> My songs of old earth's dreamy youth:
> But ah! she dreams not now; dream thou!
> For fair are poppies on the brow:
> Dream, dream, for this is also sooth.[43]

The sentiment appears somewhat artificial, but even at this time—1885—the poetic fusion of his youth with the beginning of the world suggests a Garden of Eden view of his own beginnings consonant with that in *Reveries.*

Yeats depicts an abiding but increasingly sophisticated romanticism as he grew older. He was given to wandering by himself in lonely places, and later found value in this as in his dreaming, though here too he does not always stop for explanations. He discovered a symbolical significance, for instance, in the Howth thicket where he had slept "among the rhododendrons and rocks":

There is a thicket between three roads, some distance from any of them, in the midst of Howth. I used to spend a great deal of time in that small thicket when at Howth . . . The thicket gave me my first thought of what a long poem should be. I thought of it as a region into which one should wander from the cares of life. The characters were to be no more real than the shadows that people the Howth thicket. Their mission was to lessen the solitude without destroying its peace.[44]

Later, he enjoyed seeing himself in the roles of various Shelleyan heroes, and Thoreau's *Walden* inspired his most famous dream retreat on Innisfree, the little island in Lough Gill near Sligo. His object in wanting to live on Innisfree was to attain wisdom through a romantically conceived asceticism. When he attended the art schools his romanticism became more externalized as he tried to imitate Hamlet or to assume a Byronic image, foreshadowing his assumption of poetic masks. His artistic taste, too, was romantic, but romanticism was not in fashion and his timidity forced him to keep it private.

Among his childhood dreams he focuses on those which picture him a man of action, a hero and leader of men; he was already manifesting an impulse toward all that was opposite his natural temperament, toward his anti-self. His later participation in worldly affairs would of course take a less flamboyant form than he dreamed of as a boy, but signs of independence and self-assertion are already noticeable in him at the Godolphin School. Once he had discovered how to command the respect of the other boys, he was quick to assert himself and even to assume a certain amount of leadership among them. His father had led him away from organized religion and given him a critical spirit which caused him to question values thrust upon him by educators and friends. He was guided by his experience and interests, and by the examples of people he respected. His father encouraged him in this, but J. B. Yeats's own strong opinions on all subjects soon became oppressive to a youthful spirit rebelling against parental authority. The authority of others succeeded, or at least vied with his father's, and although most were eventually set aside, it took a measure of self-assertion to repudiate them. While Yeats was absorbed in science he found his morality in the scientists. When he replaced science with poetry and occultism, he proposed that truth and morality are to be found in the writings of great poets. Public authority, however, never gained any hold over him; looked upon as an eccentric by his middle-class neighbors in Dublin he began to express contempt for the philistine mob. The contrasting environment of Dowden's home provided a refuge, and while he allowed himself to come under Dowden's authority for a time, he used it to give support to his own opinions against those of his father. When he did repudiate Dowden, he did so, not on the basis of his father's evaluation, but on his own.

His occultism, too, encouraged more self-assertion with strangers as well as with his father. Once when his former headmaster called on Dowden during the course of his own visit, for instance, Yeats shyly retired to another room; but when the same headmaster later asked him to persuade his friend Charles Johnston to leave his occult interests and return to his studies, he "had more courage," and "managed to say something about the children of this world being wiser than the children of light."[45] Yeats admits that his courage came largely out of fear, but it was courage against a seemingly venerable figure nevertheless. Shortly afterward, he attended the Contemporary Club in an attempt to overcome his shyness in public, and, determined to pursue his schooling wherever he could, forced himself to go to strange houses where he had to do without the security of intimate friends.

His confidence was further strengthened about this time, he says in the unpublished essay "How I Began," by the publication of several of his poems in the *Dublin University Review:* a little group gathered round him "whose admiration for work that had no merit justified my immense self-confidence." Yeats does not speak overtly of this emergence of confidence in *Reveries,* but it is implicit in several incidents he describes—in his encounter with his headmaster, in his many vigorous confrontations with J. F. Taylor, and in his very ambition for an Irish cultural revolution in which he himself "began to plot and scheme how one might seal with the right image the soft wax before it began to harden."[46] By the end of *Reveries* Yeats no longer appears the timid soul lost in romantic daydreams. The personal vitality which allowed him to overcome his physically delicate makeup and emotional sensitivity among the boys at the Godolphin School, to free himself even partially from the domination of his father, to defy authoritative figures like his headmaster and Dowden, to become a leader among his friends at the Hermetic Society, and to assert his own nationalist convictions in the face of so formidable a foe as J. F. Taylor, affirms the progress he was already making toward the achievement of the forceful personality of the man of action; later it would be integrated with the contemplative personality he believed was inherent in his nature.

Katharine Tynan, in her description of Yeats in *Twenty-Five Years,* saw none of this. She saw only the poet, the "precious" (an epithet which must have annoyed him) genius

separated from the world's affairs by his dreams and by his
total absorption in poetry:

> Willie Yeats was at that time of our first meeting twenty years
> old. He was tall and lanky, and his face was as you see it in that
> boyish portrait of him by his father in the Municipal Art Gallery.
> At that time he was all dreams and all gentleness. The combative
> tendencies came to him later . . . As it was—well, I daresay he had
> some consciousness of genius; and he had his dreams to interpose
> between him and the rough schoolboy world.
>
> Certainly he had not a trace of bitterness when I first knew him,
> nor for long afterwards. He was beautiful to look at with his dark
> face, its touch of vivid colouring, the night-black hair, the eager dark
> eyes. He wore a queer little beard in those days—it was just a
> little later than his father's portrait of him—and he lived, breathed,
> ate, drank, and slept poetry.
>
> I have been scolding the schoolboys; but I must acknowledge that
> in those days we all bullied Willie Yeats, I myself not excepted. I
> believe it was because *we* did not want to live, breathe, eat, drink,
> and sleep poetry: and he would have you do all those things if you
> allowed him. But then and always I knew that he was that precious
> thing to the race and the world, a genius. Driving Willie Yeats to
> and fro, I used to say to myself:
> "And did you once see Shelley plain?"[47]

Katharine Tynan seems anxious to assert her youthful intimacy with the now famous poet by pretending to feel guilty
for having bullied him when he was still too timid or gentle
to defend himself. Yet the portrait she draws is not uncompli-
mentary. It does indicate a strong will, though otherwise it
suggests none of the toughness Yeats liked to feel he had
superimposed on himself; her portrait sets out a prior and
partial image. In describing Yeats as a man who "lived,
breathed, ate, drank, and slept poetry," she gives no inkling
of the variety of concerns which, he felt, gave wholeness to
his personality. Indeed, the centering of *Reveries* so much on
this variety must have been motivated partly by a desire to

refute Katharine Tynan's charge here as he had refuted George Moore's in regard to his ancestors.

Although Yeats's life is already distinguished by a complexity of interests at the end of *Reveries,* and he is already beginning to combine characteristics of the active with those of the contemplative man, his personality was still inchoate at that time. In this sense, "It seems as if time had not yet been created," for it is the primordial development of his personality which Yeats recalls. By the end of *Reveries* all its features are plainly evident, but philosophy has yet to give them form and meaning so that they might be brought into unity, or, using Yeats's metaphor, so that to touch one musical string would be to set all the other strings vibrating. In short, they must be given form and meaning before true personality in the Yeatsian sense could be realized. Yeats concludes *Reveries* by drawing our attention back to the primal vision with which it begins when, by weighing all life in the scales of his own life, he, like Vico, discovers all human destiny in his own mind.[48]

four

THE SEARCH
FOR UNITY

Yeats came to feel that he could write with authority only if he were able to bring his many interests into conjunction. Just when the concept of unity of being first became a goal for him is uncertain. He himself, writing in 1919, said that the necessity for hammering his thoughts into unity began in 1888 or 1889.[1] The phrase "unity of being" he heard first from his father, though he attributes its conception to Dante. At the time he wrote *Reveries,* however, the concept was still unsystematic in application, and the book evolved for the most part aside from it. It was only after he began work on *A Vision* that it seemed to him he might represent his own sense of unity in the form of a system which would encompass the history of the Western world, his personal history or autobiography, and the relation between physical and metaphysical states or worlds. Not until then did the exfoliative process elucidated in *Reveries* clarify itself within the total autobiographical pattern.

Because he was preoccupied with his system of unity, the

next segment of his autobiography, *The Trembling of the Veil,* has a quite different look from *Reveries.* Instead of recounting the evolution of his thought, he now marshals together all kinds of experience—his own and that of others —to suggest how each personality failed of completeness in relation to the theory he was formulating in *A Vision* of *discordia concors,* or a harmony of opposites. In terms of the "stylistic arrangements of experience" in *A Vision,* personalities are classified into twenty-eight basic types according to the proportion of subjective to objective impulse manifested in them. Each of these archetypes corresponds metaphorically to a different phase of the lunar cycle. Phase one represents total objectivity, phase fifteen total subjectivity; neither of the totalities admit of human life, which cannot exist without conflict, though the artist constantly strives in his art—often at the expense of his life—for the perfection of the imagination embodied in phase fifteen. To oversimplify, the system prescribes that people pass through all the other phases during the course of their lives, but that their personalities are classified according to their most dominant traits during the time of their productive maturity. Those persons inclined to be more subjective (phases nine through twenty-one) instinctively seek personal fulfillment through the discovery and expression of their own true, inner selves, apprehended as the "mask" (a recondite extension of the ordinary poetic mask); those inclined to be objective (phases two through seven, and twenty-three through twenty-eight) do so through the discovery and expression of forces in the external world with which they experience a mutual influence, that is, through their "body of fate." (Phases eight and twenty-two indicate a balance, or tension, between subjective and objective impulse.) The more subjective individual finds authority in his imagination, the more objective in empirical evidence. Emotion is generally associated with subjectivity, intellect with objectivity; both are necessary to wholeness or unity, but the greatest difficulty rests in the individual's ability to discover his inner self imaged in the mask, a discovery for which the strength of personal assertion in the predominantly subjective individual is necessary. True completeness of being is impossible within the confines of human life, but an approximation of unity is conceivable—a unity like that of Dante or Shelley.

In his own case, Yeats thought he had been right in searching from childhood for a systematization of his thought which would express both its immediate concerns and its most imaginative glimpses. He therefore begins *The Trembling of the Veil* by describing his effort to make what he calls a new religion, though it is more like a new symbology:

I was unlike others of my generation in one thing only. I am very religious, and deprived by Huxley and Tyndall, whom I detested, of the simple-minded religion of my childhood, I had made a new religion, almost an infallible church of poetic tradition, of a fardel of stories, and of personages, and of emotions, inseparable from their first expression, passed on from generation to generation by poets and painters with some help from philosophers and theologians. I wished for a world, where I could discover this tradition perpetually, and not in pictures and in poems only, but in tiles round the chimney-piece and in the hangings that kept out the draft.[2]

Then he examines the inability of his friends to achieve fullness of being; from these he seeks unity in Ireland as a whole, proceeding, in effect, to treat Ireland as if it, like the persons within it, were also in quest of some meaningful totality. From Ireland he moves to consider the race, discussing with a kind of interested calm the present stage of man's spiritual evolution in relation to the *Anima Mundi*.

That Yeats was consciously formulating *The Trembling of the Veil* in this way is confirmed by his other writings. His letters to George Russell of March 14 and July 1, 1921, suggest such a plan,[3] and in December 1920 he had written Lady

Gregory that the book would be a "political and literary testament intended to give a philosophy to the movement. Every analysis of character," he says, "of Wilde, Henley Shaw and so on builds up my philosophic nationalism—it is nationalism against internationalism, the rooted against the rootless people."[4] The relation of individual lives to the life of a nation is underlined in "If I Were Four-and-Twenty," where he pretends to be too old to recommend to the nation "a new doctrine, that of unity of being."[5]

Within *The Trembling of the Veil* the first section is devoted to "Four Years: 1887-1891." Here Yeats treats of individuals but always in relation to his first principles. In his anatomy of their characters he is kindly but searching, exposing the personal inadequacies that caused most of them to lose their struggles against the hostile world he describes in "The Tragic Generation." He begins with friends of his father who became also his friends; among them John Todhunter and York Powell are exemplary. Todhunter had failed to associate himself with artistic tradition and even with his own work, so that "with him every book was a new planting, and not a new bud on an old bough."[6] York Powell lacked both special loyalties and antagonisms, which bring with them an urge to draw experiences together.

In the actress Florence Farr he finds more of the clash of opposing forces that fascinates him. Her beauty was tranquil, and classic, and her talent suited this beauty, but she valued popular opinion and spent her best years in uncertainty between fashionable and unfashionable roles. Her ambition conflicting with her genius, she was torn between conflicting ages and values. In consequence, her life became muddled as she lived in one fragment of it or another. Her personal life lacked spontaneous feeling while her art suffered from her rejection of her own genius.[7] Division was too complete for her to harmonize the conflicting forces.

In contrast to this unsuccess Yeats analyzes the apparent success of Bernard Shaw, whom he here identifies only as D—. Shaw, in spite of his flamboyant rebelliousness to traditional authority, was in harmony with his age and therefore could easily overcome its superficial hostility. But Yeats finds a hollowness in him that comes from his actually being too much in harmony with the world.[8] Without a conflict between man and age, Yeats suggests in "The Tragic Generation," where he completes the characterization, the greater feats of self-expression are impossible. Apart from expressing his own time and circumstances, Shaw had no significance, and in expressing so perfectly his age he failed to express himself. The age, moreover, was one of fragments, so that he merely reflected its disunity.

Among other writers, William Ernest Henley and Oscar Wilde, hostile to each other in life and counterposed also in death, offer Yeats one of those several examples of opposites upon which "Four Years" is largely based. While Henley had passion, he lacked the power to express it, straining instead for unnatural form and contrived attitude.[9] Strain is also evident in Wilde, where, however, it is a strain for effect, and not for one effect only but for a succession of melodramatic and imperfectly sustained effects. Insincerity and insolence were the result. He was caught among various confused and naturally contradictory projections of himself.[10]

Against these men who were torn into fragments by internal conflict Yeats poses William Morris, who felt none of their tension between the dream and actuality. Never conscious of an antithesis, Morris lived in a world without tensions. The result was to make him happy, but, because of a failure of intellectual ordering, shallow.[11] His deficiency was manifest in his literary style and in his inability to understand his own life as an expression of a larger cultural tradition. Nonetheless, the shortcomings of Morris's writing, like those of his social philosophy and of his politics, and even of his personality, could not detract from Yeats's appreciation of a kind of clairvoyance belonging uniquely to the poet, combined with the moral outlook of the social thinker and the vision of the romantic dreamer. The combination, manifested instinctively in both his life and his work, brought past, present, and future into a single ordered form notwithstanding his inability to perceive it intellectually.[12] Because of this, Yeats could not resist saying that "if some angel offered me the choice, I would choose to live his life, poetry and all, rather than my own or any other man's."[13] The statement is of course hyperbolical, since, lacking intellectual insight, Morris's personality, and consequently his work, contained a void which made true wholeness, or unity of being impossible. Personal fulfillment for Yeats had become inextricably bound up with unity of being and in this context Morris's life was a failure like the others.

In addition to Morris, Yeats discusses two other late Pre-Raphaelites, J. T. Nettleship and Edwin Ellis. Nettleship, a visionary by nature, was untrue to his vision by painting realistic lions.[14] He thereby oversimplified himself, while Ellis never succeeded in either simplifying or fixing his conception of himself. Ellis was poet, painter, and scholar but believed himself mathematician and scientist. He went from theme to theme as from love affair to love affair, always adrift.

From these literary men Yeats turns to consider some of his occultist friends. *Reveries* displays his long-developing interest in esoteric spiritual matters, and these friends appealed to him further, he says, by a defect in his own nature which was at once gregarious and avid for "proud and lonely things." He had been captivated by Ahasuerus in Shelley's "Hellas," the figure of the wandering Jew as symbol of powerful, outlawed wisdom, and so was drawn to the Theosophists who affirmed that Ahasuerus still lived.

In this state of mind Yeats sought out Madame Helena Petrovna Blavatsky in London. Although he was to quarrel with her later, her personality never disappointed him. He found in her the unpredictable abundance of personality which he so much admired, and was fascinated by her union of ancient wisdom and caprice.[15] Her disciples were deadened by abstraction, becoming mere fragments of human beings and naive objects of her derision because of it.[16] But she herself had traveled extensively, storing up vast amounts of worldly experience. Imposing upon this experience her own powerful personality and self-assurance, she had assumed a pose in which she appeared to embody the wisdom and power of Ahasuerus himself. Her only defect was a conceptual instability: unable or unwilling to systematize her thoughts, she demanded of her followers an unquestioning allegiance to a shifting dogma. Yeats soon offended her and was asked to resign from her lodge.

By this time he was already acquainted with another claimant to supernatural wisdom, MacGregor Mathers.[17] Under Mathers's tutelage Yeats found generosity and tolerance in place of Madame Blavatsky's dogmatism. His new freedom, as he indicates explicitly in "Memoirs," stimulated his imagination and ambitions: "'We only give you symbols' MacGregor Mathers had said to me 'because we respect your liberty' and now I made a curious discovery—after I had been moved by ritual, I formed plans for deeds of all kinds. I wanted to return to Ireland to find there some public work, whereas when I had returned from meetings of the esoteric section I had no thought but for more thoughts, more discussions." The congenial atmosphere did not last, however. In a short time Mathers was to balance Madame Blavatsky's erratic willfulness by an opposite infirmity, fixed obsession. Too subjective for his own good, he fell prey to delusions of grandeur.

Yeats saw clearly that he could never achieve what he hoped unless he was able to systematize his thoughts and unify them with his feelings. MacGregor Mathers was inadequate to his ambitions at least partly because he lacked an intellectual foundation for them, and it was a distinct failing of the Rhymers' Club that its members so emphatically rejected intellectual discussion. Yeats often irritated his fellow Rhymers, he says, by attempting to inject philosophy or literary theory into their discourse; a refusal to admit even the suggestion of generalization this necessarily entailed plunged their meetings into banality many times. His abiding conviction of the artist's need for an intellectual base was demonstrated several years later by his unequivocal support of the French Symbolists in their formulating a philosophical doctrine: "All writers, all artists of any kind," he says in his 1900 essay, "The Symbolism of Poetry," "in so far as they have had any philosophical or critical power, perhaps just in so far as they have been deliberate artists at all, have had some philosophy, some criticism of their art; and it has often been this philosophy, or this criticism, that has evoked their most startling inspiration, calling into outer life some portion of the divine life, or the buried reality, which could alone extinguish in the emotions what their philosophy or their criticism would extinguish in the intellect."[18] Yeats does not insist upon the intellect's providing logical or factual truth leading to a correspondingly objective philosophical doctrine; it works instead, whatever formulations it finally evolves, as a kind of catalyst which stirs the artist's imagination to discover new forms of, or the "buried" reality.

The Rhymers' Club was a failure in so far as its members refused to have "some philosophy, some criticism of their art." William Morris and Madame Blavatsky lacked intellectual perception or, as it were, convictions which spring mainly from the thoughts that "sustain us in defeat, or give us victory, whether over ourselves or others." Victory for these subjective individuals as for others must rest upon an intellectual rather than emotional confrontation of a practical and hostile world, or as Yeats has it, on "an intellectual daily recreation of all that exterior fate snatches away."[19] Life must be conceived as constant conflict. Morris and Madame Blavatsky were just as inadequate in their own way as were their followers, the Socialists and Theosophists, whose lives were consumed by their own abstract perceptions.

But the Rhymers, Morris and Madame Blavatsky were exceptions. Most of the world, in fact, was imbued with a surfeit of intellectualism, and had in consequence resolved itself into a state of abstraction that was stultifying. Since Chaucer's time the world had become increasingly fragmented: his casual blending of diverse personalities into a total microcosmic image had broken down into individual worlds revolving around each of the Elizabethan dramatic heroes,[20] and later broken down still further into the introspective obsessions of the romantic ego. Especially since the end of the seventeenth century, Yeats says, this fragmentation has with a few notable exceptions intensified the isolation of the individual both in everyday life and in art. In so doing, it has led to a deadening of the individual human spirit, which must be engaged in constant interplay with other spirits in order to maintain its vitality. Without the invigoration growing out of a mutual exchange between diverse impulses, the individual personality congeals into an existence that is an abstraction of life rather than life itself. Yeats makes clear in "Memoirs" that the absence of life's diversity was responsible for the extreme intellectual and spiritual limitations of the Theosophists. Upon being asked to resign from their lodge for conducting experiments which caused the members to be uncertain and troubled, he replied to the secretary: "By teaching an abstract system without experiment or evidence you are making your pupils dogmatic, and you are taking them out of life. There is scarcely one of your pupils who does not need more than all else to enrich his soul in the common relations of life. They do not marry and nothing is as bad for them as asceticism." Todhunter, Florence Farr, Shaw, Wilde, Henley, and the Socialists, as well as the Theosophists, were all, each in his own way, victims or manifestations of the world's movement toward this condition. It seemed possible, however, since "abstraction had reached, or all but reached its climax,"[21] for literature to reverse the process, to create images or symbols powerful enough to evoke a universal response which could give back a vital relationship between men whose worlds had become far removed from each other, and at the same time allow enough intellectual awareness to give these images and symbols authority.

This reversal implied synthesizing the fragments into which the world had fallen. "A nation or an individual," Yeats says, "with great emotional intensity might . . . give to all those separated elements, and to all that abstract love and melancholy, a symbolical, a mythological coherence." The individuals Yeats knew having failed of this power, he now turns to the nation. The uneducated rural Irishman, almost alone among his counterparts in the rest of Europe, had not moved with the world as it became more fragmented and abstract. For him the heroes and stories of Irish mythology were still real and the sacred mountains still sacred. He still combined music, speech, and dance to express himself, and was still one with the land on which he lived: "Have not all races had their first unity from a mythology, that marries them to rock and hill?"[22] It seemed possible, if artists could make known the stories and images that still held their ancient vitality among these rustic people, to build upon this foundation a culture where practical life and artistic expression have meaning for educated and uneducated alike, and thereby to bring unity to the nation. The idea of unity of culture comes in "Four Years," Yeats wrote George Russell on March 14, 1921, "after the chapters on Madame Blavatsky, Morris, Macgregor, Henley and so on and will come as a logical deduction."[23] The final pages of "Four Years," then, bring him to the need for shifting his focus from individuals to Irish tradition and culture, and thereby serve as a transition to "Ireland After Parnell" where he resumes the search for unity through his national interest.

According to Yeats's observation (and consistent with the dying Carleton's prophecy of 1869) the approximately twenty years preceding Parnell's death were devoted in Ireland to political considerations; literary interests, along with intellectual and artistic interests in general, all but ceased entirely. But the overall disenchantment that set in after the death of Parnell occasioned that "first lull in politics" in which Yeats felt a new cultural movement was possible. He had prophesied such a movement and wished to fulfill the prophecy. Furthermore, while his search for unity was necessarily limited to observation regarding his friends, he was now impelled by the possibility of actually shaping a still pliable culture according to his ideal.

Although he took up his nationalist activities with hope and enthusiasm, the Ireland Yeats describes in "Ireland After Parnell" had been torn into pieces by the political movement just ended, and especially by the turbulence which actually caused its demise; upon his entrance into its affairs Ireland was as fragmented as the individuals he describes in "Four Years." The literary movement with which he planned to fill the political vacuum, moreover, was itself divided by a heated factionalism. One faction consisted of a few young men and many older ones who joined his newly founded Irish Literary Society in London or National Literary Society in Dublin because they were nostalgic for the Young Ireland movement of the 1840's and 1850's. These men gathered round Sir Charles Gavan Duffy upon his return from Australia, where he had attained political eminence after having left Ireland in 1855, in total despair for its fate. Duffy had been a Young Ireland leader and in 1842, along with Thomas Davis and John Blake Dillon, had founded *The Nation,* a nationalist newspaper. The movement under his direction, absorbed in patriotic sentiment and moral politics, and still obsessed with Young Ireland images of forty years before, would be turned into everything Yeats found commonplace, dogmatic, and shabby in Irish nationalism. Duffy, Yeats believed, was devoted to chauvinist ideals that were uncritical, without sincere emotion, and entirely different from Yeats's own notions of national unity. "I am characterizing Hyde, AE, O'Grady, Lionel," he wrote to Olivia Shakespear on August 1, 1921, "and characterizing, without naming, my especial enemies, the Tower and wolf-dog, harp and shamrock, verdigris-green sectaries who wrecked my movement for the time."[24] Yeats himself led the other faction. He was quickly becoming convinced that the most direct road to a significant literature, and then to national unity, lay opposite that which the others were taking, that is, in satire and criticism rather than praise. "Original virtue arises from the discovery of evil," and hence the nation's greatest liabilities, if "declared and measured," could be turned into its greatest assets.[25] This view must indeed have appeared a perverse form of patriotism to Duffy's Young Irelanders.

The movement was still further divided. Yeats's theory was not likely to be popular, and many opposed Duffy on political or other grounds. Most moved toward Duffy, but divisions in the ranks of both leaders were numerous. Even men upon whom Yeats relied deserted him, either because of self-interest, honest disagreement, or what Yeats attributed to a universal trend toward mediocrity. In addition, groups and

individuals contributed to the fragmentation by being preoccupied with their own special interests—folklore, politics,
language, morality, occultism, or the like. The diversity of
these interests in certain ways injected real vitality into the
movement, but they, along with the various ideological and
political schisms, also made it even more divided as it pro-
gressed than it was at its outset.

Yeats uses John O'Leary and John F. Taylor to exemplify
and to polarize the basic ideological controversy between
Duffy and himself that divided the literary movement from
the start. O'Leary sided with Yeats whenever he was convinced
there was no individual moral laxity, morality for him being
determined by objective evaluation of each individual action.
His standard was based on a measure of excellence. Despite
his discipleship under O'Leary, Taylor, for whom immorality
was associated indiscriminately with everything that he felt
brought discredit to Ireland, violently disagreed with Yeats.
Yeats "had published Irish folk-lore in English reviews to the
discredit . . . of the Irish peasantry, and . . . England within
earshot . . . found fault with the Young Ireland prose and
poetry."[26] Though his motives were sincere, Taylor, like so
many others of his inclination, would have had no inkling
had he lived long enough to see it, that a play like Synge's
Playboy of the Western World could contribute so greatly to
Ireland's dignity simply by being good art. He vigorously supported Duffy, and was in turn, to Yeats's embarrassment, supported by Maud Gonne.[27]

Yeats gives Douglas Hyde, Standish O'Grady, and Lionel
Johnson roles as distinguished Irish writers (the last, to be
sure, an adopted son of Ireland) who further contributed to
the movement's division, although their contributions were
undoubtedly more often efficacious than harmful. Yeats's distinction between division and diversity often appears rather
finely drawn.

Hyde's early treatment of Irish folklore actually created a medium of understanding between uneducated peasant and educated urbanite that was a valuable contribution to the national unity Yeats was seeking. The understanding was subconscious, but his Irish songs sung by working Connacht peasants ignorant of whose words they were singing brought peasant and poet into a relationship that was an exemplar of Yeats's idea of unity of culture. This work was never undone. Yet it was not long until the public, Yeats's constant antagonist, drove Hyde into the political maneuvering that pervaded the literary movement, and eventually into forming the Gaelic League. In literary politics he was "Yeats's man," and the Gaelic League brought a new, if divisive dimension to the movement. But these activities cut him off from the area where his genius could most effectively be fulfilled, in giving artistic form to native emotion and instinct.[28] In consequence, an important potential force for national unity was dissipated.

Standish O'Grady brought to the movement a quarrelsome spirit and a series of contradictions within his own nature, but also an eloquence that increased with argument and opposition. Lionel Johnson was the movement's critic, according to Yeats, and he brought to it his own form of passionate and sensitive eccentricity. He became very devout, castigating sinners and heretics and advocating the most extreme asceticism, while at the same time virtually drinking himself to death; he displayed a kind of boisterous serenity at having achieved certainty in religious belief, and suffered torments of a confused identity.

Hyde, O'Grady, and Johnson, O'Leary and possibly even Taylor contributed elements of diversity which were inevitable if the nation was to have the breadth and depth implicit in Yeats's concept of wholeness.[29] But the diverse interests and perspectives had somehow to be made compatible. Political if not total unity had previously been inspired by the all-pervading image of Parnell. With this image shattered (or existing, if at all, as a disruptive force) unity had to be inspired by a universal desire for excellence and a generosity of spirit.[30]

This was not to be the case. The movement, and even the characteristic, winning irrationality and exorbitance of manner springing from the naturally deep-feeling, spontaneous Irish temperament that Yeats delighted in, were stifled by mediocre minds and narrow visions. Devotion to abstract principles was so devoid of intellect and strengthened by trumped-up emotion that no diversity was tolerated by either side in any argument. Trying to keep nationalist support while attacking "so much that seemed sacred to Irish nationalist opinion,"[31] Yeats finds that he himself was driven to a nationalist fanaticism characterized by a paucity of both intellect and sincere emotion, and thus to an antithetical state of mind so contradictory as to make reconciliation with his natural self impossible. In this he reflected in his own person, as it were, the condition of the nation as a whole, and lost, or never made, friendships which he might have valued both personally and for the unity of culture he was seeking.[32]

Against all these forces of division, Yeats poses one man who was capable of bringing the divided elements into closer harmony. George Russell, like O'Leary, was a great moralist; he was equally able to understand and sympathize with both sides of an argument, and his sense of justice, accompanied by the capacity to delineate an issue with perfect clarity, was perhaps more profound than O'Leary's. His depth of vision, moreover, had commanded respect, indeed veneration, even when Yeats first knew him at the art schools. Hence, his powerful moral nature, strengthened by his extraordinary sense of justice, clarified by his aptitude for expression, and made recondite by his vision, made him "the one masterful influence among young Dublin men and women who love religious speculation, but have no historical faith,"[33] and his work in the practical world eventually gave him influence among those whose lives had little to do with spiritual life.

Yeats concedes Russell's valuable talents, but nonetheless finds him severely limited as an effective personality. His image as presented in "Ireland After Parnell" is that of the religious sage, an image he had assumed, Yeats says, not by creating it out of his inner self, but by having it imposed upon him by his followers. Yeats placed him at phase twenty-five in the lunar scheme of *A Vision*. The man of phase twenty-five is the "conditional man," "conditional" because "all the man's thought arises out of some particular condition of actual life, or is an attempt to change that condition through social conscience."[34] In other words, whatever effectiveness his personality exerts on others comes not out of its innate power but out of the reaction of his mind to pressures of the external world. He, like other men of his phase, is made strong to the extent that he can exert an effect upon his contemporaries; specifically in Russell's case to the extent that he can impose order, justice and goodness upon them.

His strength so acquired constituted the "religious genius" that infuriated Yeats when he met it in connection with art.[35] The nature of "religious genius" is that it lacks the power of artistic discrimination and that its best expression is inspired by others or occurs in philosophical propaganda. When Russell turned to his inner self for inspiration his work became imitative. This is strongly implied in "Ireland After Parnell," but made explicit in *A Vision*:

Every poem, where he is moved to write by some form of philosophical propaganda, is precise, delicate and original, while in his visionary painting one discovers the influence of other men, Gustave Moreau, for instance. This painting is like many of his "visions," an attempt to live in the *Mask*, caused by critical ideas founded upon *antithetical* art. What dialect was to Synge, his practical work as a cooperative organiser was to him, and he found precise ideas and sincere emotion in the expression of conviction. He learned practically, but not theoretically, that he must fly the *Mask*. His work should neither be consciously aesthetic nor consciously speculative but imitative of a central Being—the *Mask* as his pursuer—consciously apprehended as something distinct, as something never imminent though eternally united to the soul.[36]

There could be no unity of being for Russell since there could be no becoming one with the mask, the image of his true, inner self. Instead, he had to find unity outside himself, but in so doing he did his best work for Ireland. Because he could find the unities of the external world, his effect upon Ireland during these years ran counter to that of more subjective men: he imposed unity while they imposed multiplicity.

But Russell was inadequate to the significant advancement of Yeats's ideal, because if Ireland were to achieve real unity of culture at all, it would be able to do so only when those who dominated its society had arrived at some measure of unity within themselves. "Politics," Yeats says, "for a vision-seeking man, can be but half achievement, a choice of an almost easy kind of skill instead of that kind which is, of all those not impossible, the most difficult."[37] Russell's "religious genius" imposed unity so far as it could, but this genius being limited, and his influence being less far reaching than Parnell's, he could scarcely be expected to succeed where Parnell himself had failed. Every area of Irish activity, whether intellectual, spiritual, artistic, or political, was separated from every other and internally divided. Ireland remained, notwithstanding Russell's "religious genius," Yeats's work and the work of his other friends, a "bundle of fragments."

Yeats sought unity, then, first among individuals he knew, then in the nation as a whole. He had suggested the possibility of its attainment through art at the end of "Four Years," and, because he confined it to a national art in order that it not be "rootless," his interests in art and Irish nationalism were brought together. But the pursuance of unity through his nationalist efforts, while not hopeless, was for the time unrewarding. In "Hodos Chameliontos" he extends his horizon still further by turning, now with a deeper philosophical bearing, to the total cultural evolution of the race.

He indicates that he was originally inspired to do this by his discovery of an uninhabited island castle in Lough Kay. The "Castle on the Rock," romantically isolated in the middle of its lake and enclosed all round by a beautiful land permeated with reminders of Irish mythology and folklore, suggested to him a retreat for a mystical Order which would be served by the allied powers of literature and national consciousness, and which for its part would strengthen the literary revival and nationalist movement with intellectual and spiritual support. Members of the Order would have the opportunity to retire from the everyday practical world to an atmosphere that was beautiful, serene, and inspiring, where they could meditate and read books on Irish art, history, and myth, and to these would be added books of philosophy and the occult. Such a venture would unite all Yeats's major interests. But while he had settled rather definitely on the directions art and Irish nationalism were to take, philosophy, beyond a general desire for unity, still eluded him. Yet, he describes having had "an unshakable conviction" that philosophy eventually would come, and would do so through some form of preternatural intervention.

His conviction was based on precedents in the lives of Blake, Swedenborg, and Boehme. Blake's greatest work, Yeats recalls in an essay of 1897, began the moment he " 'was again enlightened with the light . . . enjoyed in . . . youth, and which . . . [had] for exactly twenty years been closed from . . . [him], as by a door and by window-shutters.' "[38] "Divine Mystery," he says in 1914, began to be revealed to Swedenborg when, "in his fifty-eighth year . . . a spirit appeared before him who was, he believed, Christ himself, and told him that henceforth he could commune with spirits and angels."[39] Boehme had asserted "that imagination was the first emanation of divinity, 'the body of God,' 'the Divine members.' "[40] Yeats believed that for himself, too, philosophy would be revealed as with the opening of "invisible gates."

The need for ritual in his mystical Order was, after MacGregor Mathers's influence, a foregone conclusion. Ritual, Yeats says somewhat vaguely in "Memoirs," was "to re-unite the perception of the spirit, of the dream, with natural beauty." When speaking of ritual, or ceremony, Yeats often has in mind a broader meaning associated with an entire mode of living, but one which—lifting man from his common, primitive state by appealing to emotions arising out of cultivated sensibilities—is related to the more ordinary religious kind he always considered necessary in connection with occult practice. He describes in "Hodos Chameliontos" having used Mathers's teaching as a starting point and then having spent several years with the help of friends, not deliberately formulating ritual as he would a poem, but trying by meditation and the use of symbol to create an atmosphere whereby ritual would be revealed like the philosophy itself. He had been experiencing visions since childhood, but for his present purpose he set out deliberately to find a kind of visionary synthesis.

Almost from the beginning, Yeats's experiments indicated that images could be evoked easily enough and often with surprising clarity, but he was frustrated because they were almost always fragmented and enigmatical. To understand the nature and meaning of these images became an obsession. What could be the source of an image that had no connection with the viewer's experience? Then again, what was it that brought two or more minds, as often happened, into an unpredictable working intimacy? Yeats had no evidence, he says, but he found a useful solution in the concept of a great universal memory or mind independent of individual memories and minds, but containing the accumulation of all their images and thoughts. He knew this universal, or mythic memory most specifically as the *Anima Mundi* described by the seventeenth-century neoplatonic philosopher Henry More. As Ellmann explains Yeats's use of the *Anima Mundi,* each individual in drawing upon the cumulative great memory (mind or imagination—the terms are used interchangeably) does so within the range of his own vision. In a very real sense, then, each individual freshly creates the external world around him, and there are "as many external worlds as there are imaginative men to create them." Yeats conceives of the *Anima Mundi* as a corporate imagination which includes all individual imaginations and hence all images and ideas, or worlds, arising out of them, "and the man who is able to let his imagination fuse with this corporate imagination has all the images ever wrought by men available to him as well as the power to create new ones."[41] Although Yeats says little in "Hodos Chameliontos" about the *Anima Mundi* directly, perhaps because he had already discussed it at length in earlier essays, it becomes the underlying premise of all his discoveries.

He had explained its function in his essay on "Magic" in 1901. Our individual minds, he said, "flow into one another" to form a single great mind, our memories "are a part of one great memory, the memory of Nature herself," and "this great mind and great memory can be evoked by symbols."[42] Even earlier, in his 1900 essay on Shelley, he had described "our little memories" as "but a part of some great Memory that renews the world and men's thoughts age after age," and contended that "our thoughts are not, as we suppose, the deep, but a little foam upon the deep."[43] The metaphor recurs in *Per Amica Silentia Lunae* of 1917: "Our daily thought was certainly but the line of foam at the shallow edge of a vast luminous sea; Henry More's *Anima Mundi,* Wordsworth's 'immortal sea which brought us hither,' and near whose edge the children sport, and in that sea there were some who swam or sailed, explorers who perhaps knew all its shores."[44]

Within the corporate imagination or great memory artificial human distinctions disappear; individual minds and memories flow into one another in this "vast luminous sea." Economic and educational differences are dissolved as well as those between the wise man and the fool, between the philosopher, artist, and mathematician. The living and the dead are reunited, and because both had existed as reality in the minds of men, history and myth become indistinguishable.[45] The natural instincts of children and even of animals, moreover, originate in the great memory. All images of godhead reside there, of Christ and of the antichrist that "Slouches towards Bethlehem to be born," as do, finally, the images of our own true, inner selves. The *Anima Mundi* includes all images of all minds.

The problem, Yeats demonstrates, was to penetrate it. Communication with the universal memory is occasionally possible for the individual, he says, through an association of thoughts, images, and objects, but it is at any time extremely difficult. He was searching, with a kind of Faustian impulse, for an image which would in "some moment of passionate experience" reveal the truth underlying the illusions of the visible world. Upon this truth, which would be a concentration of the race's accumulated truth, the quintessence of its culture as it were, unity of culture could be built. But all attempts to bring about an enduring synthesis failed. The individual living man appeared to be incapable of evoking images from the great memory in compliance with his will, these images being amorphous, incomprehensible, desultory, and mutable. "But now image called up image in an endless procession," he says, "and I could not always choose among them with any confidence; and when I did choose, the image lost its intensity, or changed into some other image . . . I was lost in that region a cabalistic manuscript, shown me by MacGregor Mathers, had warned me of; astray upon the Path of the Chamelion, upon *Hodos Chameliontos*."[46] Yeats has it that the individual is separated from the *Anima Mundi* by the temporal world in which he lives, much as Plato has him separated from the Eternal Essences and Wordsworth has him separated from God. Ordinarily, except for the instincts with which he is endowed before birth, and certain instances of momentary revelation, he cannot directly share in the wisdom and experience accumulated in the great memory throughout the ages.

Because the individual is separated at birth from the *Anima Mundi,* which contains among the rest his true but buried self, his life begins in a fragmented condition, and can be made whole only by an almost impossible reunification. There are, however, "personifying spirits" ("Gates and Gate-keepers") whose only concern is to confer now and then upon a certain chosen man having extraordinary powers of concentration and imagination the gift of genius, which Yeats says is a "crisis that joins that buried self for certain moments to our trivial daily mind." They do this by bringing him, through passion rather than intellectual contemplation, "to the greatest obstacle he may confront without despair." In a temporal context this is to heighten his emotional capacities and extend his wisdom—both of which in the selected man are already of extraordinary power—by straining them to their utmost limits, that is by depriving him of what appears most congenial to his nature and by immersing him in its opposite, by contriving Dante's banishment from Florence and by snatching away his Beatrice, or by thrusting "Villon into the arms of harlots." Dante "celebrated the most pure lady poet ever sung and the Divine Justice, not merely because death took that lady and Florence banished her singer, but because he had to struggle in his own heart with his unjust anger and his lust."[47] In a spiritual context it is to remove the illusions of the visible world and confront him directly with his mask, the image of his ideal self, which is his opposite or anti-self since it eliminates all the deficiencies that he recognizes in his ordinary personality. Confrontation of the mask can be accomplished only by raising the mind to its highest pitch.

The difficulty is that the confrontation must not be sought consciously, but instinctively, for success comes through revelation. The temporal or primary self, viewed through the distorted perspective of each individual, is a mirrored reflection of the true self, and is, therefore, as a reflection is an inverted image of the reflected object, an inverted image. Hence, the true self is antithetical to the primary self, and Yeats refers to it as the antithetical self. The mask, on the other hand, is the true rather than the reflected image of the antithetical self and so also the primary self's antithesis. When one seeks his mask, then, he really seeks an image out of *Anima Mundi,* an image, moreover, which is free of the subjective distortions of the individual's primary perspective. But the antithetical self alone does not, any more than the primary self, represent wholeness. There must be a blending of primary and antithetical, of objective and subjective impulses. The needed confrontation of primary self and mask is a human crisis brought about through immense personal anguish, producing an almost unbearable emotional tension in the individual, but effecting the union of self and anti-self, or of primary and antithetical selves. Only with primary self and mask made one is the way opened for the primary self to become joined with the antithetical self residing in *Anima Mundi,* and an approximation of wholeness, or unity of being, achieved.[48]

The measure of an artist's greatness depends largely upon the explosive conjunction of his primary with his antithetical self, upon the measure of unity of being he achieves in his work. That of Dante and Villon, to use Yeats's examples again, is greater than that of Keats and Landor (who ranks curiously high in Yeats's system). Great art is not merely created out of the conjunction of the artist's mind and the external world, but rather out of the artist's denial of his primary self and the re-creation of his mask, the true image of his antithetical self and a fragment of the *Anima Mundi.* In recreating this fragment he actually creates a higher order of reality than the visible world possesses. "When I think of any great poetical writer of the past," Yeats says in *Per Amica Silentia Lunae,* "I comprehend, if I know the lineaments of his life, that the work is the man's flight from his entire horoscope, his blind struggle in the network of the stars."[49] In denying his primary self (to which his horoscope belongs) in favor of his antithetical self, he merely denies an inverted image in favor of his real self.

The very notion of denial, however, seems to contradict that of becoming one with the mask, of blending self and mask. How, after all, can two elements be blended if one is denied to begin with? In fact, denial, as Yeats uses the term here, implies not so much negation as restraint from assertion of the primary self; the artist instinctively creates a reflection (an inverted image) of his primary self, or a true image of his antithetical self. The subjective, or antithetical artist, therefore, who finds inspiration in the relationship of his primary to his antithetical self is more likely to achieve unity than the objective, or primary artist who finds it in the relationship of his primary self to the external, or visible world.

This is because the visible world is, like the primary self that lives in it, a distorted reflection of reality rather than reality itself or even a true image of it.

In "Hodos Chameliontos" Yeats gives a sense of the antithetical artist's crisis as he attempts to recreate reality: "We gaze at such men in awe," he says, "because we gaze not at a work of art, but at the re-creation of the man through that art, the birth of a new species of man, and, it may even seem that the hairs of our heads stand up, because that birth, that re-creation, is from terror."[50] Yeats was pleased when he found in his writing evidence of the simplicity of his own phase three mask, since this was evidence that he had penetrated to the reality of *Anima Mundi*.

> I call to the mysterious one who yet
> Shall walk the wet sands by the edge of the stream
> And look most like me, being indeed my double,
> And prove of all imaginable things
> The most unlike, being my anti-self,
> And, standing by these characters, disclose
> All that I seek.[51]

Aware of the futility of an intellectually contrived confrontation, the poet is limited to a yearning "call" to his anti-self, which alone can give him a glimpse into the hidden reality. There can be no total fulfillment of potential genius, no union of primary and antithetical selves, until intellect and passion together have been stretched to their utmost capacities. Then life will have arrived at the dramatic crisis wherein, possibly, the "invisible gates" will swing open.

The nation as well as the individual can achieve unity only by seeking a confrontation with its anti-self. By implication, the clashes of diverse interests within Ireland, the meeting of every idea with its opposite, might yet move the nation closer to the crisis wherein its full potential will be realized and its culture exalted. To this extent, the artist can do his country greater service through satire and criticism than through indiscriminate praise.

Yeats's mystical Order never materialized, and after having used it as a point of departure for this part of his autobiography he does not return to the subject. Alex Zwerdling maintains that "the plan suggests the necessity of divorcing oneself completely from the actual world in order to find the spiritual one."[52] Yeats himself never expressed this idea, but it does not seem unreasonable to suppose that as he became more committed to a worldliness in both his life and his art, he grew at least partially disenchanted with his plan for an Order which necessarily involved removing its members from "the common relations of life." In the process of trying to establish the Order's philosophical foundation, however, he discovered the *Anima Mundi* as a means, first, to combine his interests by giving spiritual authority to his nationalist impulses, thereby encompassing both occultism and nationalism as subject matter to be forged into poetic symbol; second, to enlarge the dimensions of the individual personality; and third, to conceptualize the hidden reality as a goal to be attained by penetrating through the illusory surface of things. Full awareness of these implications of the *Anima Mundi* came to Yeats, he says, years after the events he recounts in "Hodos Chameliontos." But even with his initial inkling, which did occur during this time, that the *Anima Mundi* was relevant as some kind of explanation of his mystical experience, he was already on the way to achieving far more than he had in any of his previous efforts to give his thoughts and feelings the ardent relationship prerequisite to unity of being.

five

THE TREMBLING

OF THE VEIL

"The Tragic Generation" appears to concentrate, like "Four Years," on the fragmentation of the individual personality, on the professional failures and messed-up lives of certain individuals because of their inability to achieve fullness or unity of being. In the two sections subsequent to "Four Years," however, Yeats has enlarged the perspective, first extending it to the nation, in "Ireland After Parnell," and again to the evolution of the race, as it accumulates experience, knowledge, and images, in "Hodos Chameliontos." The individual, seen in relation to his country and the *Anima Mundi,* appears within a much more comprehensive framework than that of "Four Years"; in "The Tragic Generation" this framework is enlarged still further to include the present stage of the world's spiritual evolution—also represented metaphorically by the lunar cycle. Now the individual life becomes a phenomenon of this evolutionary movement, notably serving to dramatize Yeats's lunar system, not only in the individual cycle, but, viewing the whole generation of artists, in a larger historical cycle as well.

Yeats says in *A Vision* that the period from 1875 to 1927 comes at phase twenty-two of an historical cycle; the same cycle included the fifteenth-century Renaissance at phase seventeen, where the relation of subjective to objective impulse makes unity of being most accessible. In the fifteenth century, he elucidates in "The Tragic Generation," "men attained to personality in great numbers, 'Unity of Being' . . . and as men so fashioned held places of power, their nations had it too, prince and ploughman sharing that thought and feeling."[1] Afterwards, subjective strength began to diminish with the infusion of constantly increasing proportions of objectivity and abstraction, until the last quarter of the nineteenth century brought abstract thought to a climax and raised objective strength to the level of phase twenty-two where the cycle passes back from the antithetical to the primary phases, from a predominance of subjectivity or personal assertion to objectivity or personal passivity. Before this time the creative mind in most men had assisted the will to become one with the mask, a condition wherein strength is lodged within the individual; after it the creative mind encourages the will to flee the mask and identify itself with the body of fate, to take whatever strength it can from the external world, and allow itself to be dominated by it.

In *A Vision* Yeats identifies the climax of abstraction, arriving at phase twenty-two, with *Hodos Chameliontos*: "Abstraction which began at Phase 19 will end at Phase 25," he says. "Our generation has witnessed a first weariness, has stood at the climax, at what in *The Trembling of the Veil* I call *Hodos Chameliontos,* and when the climax passes will recognise that there common secular thought began to break and disperse."[2] Phase twenty-two embraces, then, an upper limit which upon being reached turns men back in a new direction, and some less adaptable men become lost in the turning. Shaken suddenly into a new awareness they give up trying to remake the world and become fixed in contemplation of it. A few, Yeats continues, even doubt that there can be any synthesis; they doubt the very existence of common experience and the possibility of science. In *The Trembling of the Veil* itself, the identification of *Hodos Chameliontos* focuses more directly upon the state of frustration found in certain creative individuals when they become convinced at the outset of their careers that fruitful intercourse with the external world is impossible. The world having arrived at the phase twenty-two shift from subjective to objective values, a large number of artists were forced to turn away from it and to seek images wholly within themselves. In so doing they lost the world entirely, finding themselves, as Yeats himself did while obsessed in his own abstract attempt to penetrate the *Anima Mundi,* astray upon *Hodos Chameliontos.*

Yeats says that he never found a full explanation for the tragedy of the nineties, that he is uncertain whether to blame the tragedy that came out of his friends' divided lives on the individuals themselves, for pursuing antithesis, or on their lack of coherence because the age was in transition.[3] He does move toward a solution in both these interrelated areas, however, if not in practical or scientific terms, at least in the terms of his mythology. This twofold solution is the informing principle of "The Tragic Generation." Yeats sees, first, a paralysis of the will fixed in contemplation of its anti-self and therefore unable to associate itself creatively with the external world, and, second, a conflict between the subjective artist and the more objectively oriented phase twenty-two age in which he lives, as inevitable tragic issues of the lunar cycle.

In so abstract an historical phase, and one that is so impelled toward objective values as it moves into the primary

half of the cycle, Bernard Shaw (phase twenty-one) is relatively at home, realist novelists George Moore (also phase
twenty-one) and Zola, and realist playwright Ibsen achieve
great success; literary realism requires an objective outlook.
But the subjective artist who is concerned mainly with the
expression of his inner self, and who is himself under the
spell of phase twenty-two, comes to frustration, failure, and
despair in his abstract search for his mask, a search which
simply cannot be carried on abstractly with any chance of
success. Some of Yeats's friends, it is true, found images of
what appeared to be their own opposites. But however at
variance with their primary natures these images appeared to
be, there had been no penetration of the *Anima Mundi,*
which alone could make wholeness possible by the primary
self's subsequent union with the anti-self discovered there.
The wholeness that comes with the union of self and anti-
self brings with it a strength that the fragmented individual
cannot have, but the "Gates or Gate-keepers" guide very few
men to the crisis that makes this wholeness possible, and never
those who consciously seek it. Geniuses are rare, and never
manufactured. Those not favored must accommodate their
personalities as best they can to their age if they are to attain
any measure of serenity in their lives. But compromise is always difficult for the subjective artist, and especially so with
an age that is objective and almost inhumanly abstract.
Furthermore, lacking real communion with the external world,
the subjective artist becomes helplessly victimized in his struggle by a hostile society that hates him because he looks not
to it but to himself in determining the direction of his life
and work.

We have already examined the characterizations Yeats
completes at the beginning of "The Tragic Generation."
Todhunter was mentally estranged from the world, Henley
was obsessed in finding identity with a preconceived image,

and Wilde and Florence Farr were torn violently between conflicting images and values. The result in each instance was a personality so mechanically divided that unity was impossible. Shaw on the other hand triumphed over his age because he was in harmony with it; but the triumph rested too heavily upon a single historical phase and would be nullified by history when the world passed into the next phase. With the further delineation of these figures Yeats again takes up the characterology begun in "Four Years" and continued somewhat less overtly in "Ireland After Parnell," but set aside for the more introspective and recondite searchings of "Hodos Chameliontos." In "The Tragic Generation," however, the individuality of each character is set against the characterization of the age itself.

In Lionel Johnson, Yeats says in "Memoirs," "more than all others one can study the tragedy of this generation." "The Tragic Generation" portrays Johnson's life in terms of the antitheses with which it was imbued: his cloistered existence among his books, and his imaginary conversations with prominent people—the consequence of what Yeats believed to be a half-conscious desire for the world he had renounced; his erudition that in spite of its great range he felt it necessary to exaggerate, and his ever increasing obsession with his own feelings; his religious asceticism accompanied by sexual abstinence, and his alcoholic dissipation. Pointing up the internal conflict still further, Yeats suggests that Johnson shared with Dante a capacity for saintliness combined with a vision of evil. Dante, however, resolved the conflicting parts of his nature—the saintliness and the wickedness, his self and anti-self—into unity. The two parts struggled continuously within Johnson for possession of his soul; he was devoted to one and fascinated by the other, and finally gave in to the fascination while all the time proclaiming the purity of his devotion. Dante had been led "to the greatest obstacle he may confront without despair"; Johnson, lost and bewildered between the opposing forces within him, was in the end overcome by despair.

In his inner conflict Johnson was typical of a whole group of artists who by their introspective obsessions brought further complications to their own personalities. The doctrine of the Rhymers' Club, in so far as there was a doctrine at all, "was that lyric poetry should be personal. That a man should express his life and do this without shame or fear."[4] But Yeats makes clear in "The Tragic Generation" that the Rhymers were too much obsessed with their own emotional lives, and with pure beauty in their art: Johnson contended that everything of importance had already been said years earlier, Symons declared himself concerned only with impressions, and some of Dowson's poems "were not speech but perfect song."[5]

All considerations that would have given these poets communion with the outside world—Browning's psychology, Shelley's politics, the moral preoccupations of Wordsworth and Tennyson, or even the literary theory of the French Symbolists—were rejected out of hand.[6] Yeats does not endorse these interests as legitimate motives for poetry—he even objects vehemently to their intrusion at all except as symbols—but for the Rhymers meaningful objective life was almost totally lacking. On the other hand, their attempt to achieve pure beauty by uniting perfection of thought and feeling with perfection of form resulted in a subjectivity that took them beyond the ordinary self toward a confrontation with the ideal self. This confrontation might be likened to Kierkegaard's final "leap" into the third sphere of existence where all convention that guides thought and action is left behind.[7] Yeats has described just such a sphere of existence (but one that replaces God's authority with the individual's own passions) as a wilderness into which entry requires a measure of courage equal to that of Kierkegaard's Abraham, since here too the "elect and chosen souls" that enter achieve a kind of sanctity:

To renounce perplexities, interests, everything contemporaneous, journalistic, all that moral zeal which never fails to buy popularity, to give up everything but the inmost life of thought and passion, that was what my generation sought, that is why they were accursed. They had gone into the wilderness to find it is the beginning of sanctity . . . The Wilderness is full of wild beasts, the passions become infinite and powerful energy because they are no longer controlled and limited by circumstance and habit, but must be faced in the depth of the mind. To enter into the mind, to renounce all but the mind or what excites it to its highest intensity, that is the toil of the saint and the lyric poet. But all those passions which the saint may at last tame the poets need in their wildness.[8]

The poet differs from the saint in his desire to communicate his feelings to others, but he shares with him an attitude of complete indifference to public response. Yeats had written that much of Johnson's poetry "mirrors a temperament so cold, so austere, so indifferent to our pains and pleasures, so wrapped up in one lonely and monotonous mood that one comes from it wearied and exalted."[9] Such an indifference, whether expressed by the saint or the poet, will not be tolerated by civilized society.

The wilderness metaphor does not appear in "The Tragic Generation," having been replaced by the historical cycle of the lunar system, but it helps to clarify this more complex metaphor which underlies the events of the nineties as Yeats sees them. In the wilderness as upon *Hodos Chameliontos* the individual searches for the image of his anti-self, and the untamed thoughts and passions of the wilderness, like the images that populate *Hodos Chameliontos,* frustrate him in their elusiveness. Yet all enforce his individuality and are different from those images society as a whole finds and turns into convention. This is why society cannot tolerate the individual who goes off on his own. It is, nonetheless, only by entering the wilderness, purging away conventional values in favor of those created from the depth of his own mind, that the poet may discover his anti-self and, subsequently, that the hidden reality might be recreated or, as it were, Mallarmé's Sacred Book be written.

In the nineties a group of poets and artists were willing to make that excursion into the wilderness, and it looked as if the first "trembling of the veil of the Temple" was imminent, that the sanctified reality would be discovered by rending the veil of illusion. Johnson and Dowson, whose lives were out of keeping with conventional social prescription, were among those who turned inward to their own minds and passions in their search for truth and for the completion of their beings. But to achieve this wholeness they had to penetrate the *Anima Mundi* and discover their masks. Victims of the abstractness of phase twenty-two, and totally lacking an objective relationship with the external world, they were unable to complete their personalities and were doomed from the start to become lost among the confusions and contradictions of *Hodos Chameliontos.*

Although the tragedy of the nineties could be studied in Lionel Johnson, not all the poets of that decade attained the sanctity of the wilderness. Yeats sets up a contrasting figure in Arthur Symons, who was not subjective and who derived his inspiration from the external world. He found it in the music halls and other forms of popular entertainment, and in numerous love affairs notable for their exoticism and variety; where it did not come naturally, he contrived worldly and romantic experience for the sake of his art. His conversation with artists in London (especially with Yeats it appears) and with Symbolist poets in Paris gave him the foundation of his ideas and criticism. Once cut off by marriage from these sources of inspiration, Yeats says, his work lost its curiosity and animation. His objective nature, however, gave him a certain amount of very real success: it made possible his impressionistic studies, his sensitive translations, and his campaign as editor of *The Savoy* against the conventions of Victorian respectability. There was no possibility of unity of being for Symons as there was none for George Russell, but his objective nature protected him at least partially from the destructiveness of his age. Although he became temporarily insane (thereby acquiring his credentials as a member of the tragic generation) he eventually recovered to lead a productive, if uninspired life.

Yeats finds in Aubrey Beardsley, on the other hand, another exemplar of the subjective artist victimized by a morally obsessed society. Like Dante, and like Johnson and Dowson, Beardsley had and was fascinated by a personal vision of evil that demanded expression. His sister (Mabel Beardsley, the heroine of Yeats's poem "Upon A Dying Lady") had told Yeats during her long last illness that her brother "hated the people who denied the existence of evil, and so being young he filled his pictures with evil. He had a passion for reality."[10] Yeats placed him in lunar phase thirteen, where "the self discovers, within itself, while struggling with the *Body of Fate,* forms of emotional morbidity which others recognise as their own; as the Saint may take upon himself the physical diseases of others."[11] He expressed this morbidity in his art and at times in his life, but his own keen moral nature was outraged. The conflict raged within him as it did within Johnson, but whereas Johnson's conflict was public, blazoned in a mixture of pious conviction and drunken raving, Beardsley's morality, except in isolated painfully introspective moments, was concealed under a facade of complete degeneracy.

Beardsley's art, springing from some impersonal force that had replaced an emotion exhausted by conflict, came without desire or meditation. Yeats sees in it a satirical expression of his own disillusionment; Beardsley was the "first satirist of the soul English art has produced."[12] But art, unlike the artist, cannot take on "victimage." Beardsley, who had created a compelling beauty out of a spirit of mockery, conjured up in the public feelings of its own guilt, and the public hated him for doing so.

The artists of the nineties, Yeats says, all artists at all times for that matter, had multiple personalities. The world, passing into the primary phases, compelled the antithetical artist more than ever to fuse the divided elements within him into some kind of unity if he were to survive in it. Most remained divided. John Davidson had passion, but his intellectual receptivity was not sufficient to objectify it. His talent was quickly consumed by an overriding and undisciplined emotional energy. William Sharp's personality was so divided between himself and his alter ego, Fiona Macleod, that he was virtually psychotic. And Paul Verlaine, between that side of him responsible for his sacred poems and that responsible for his "amoral" life and sordid last days, "alternated between the two halves of his nature with so little apparent resistance that he seemed like a bad child."[13] Verlaine too might be counted with those who had achieved the sanctity of the wilderness.

The passage on Verlaine in "The Tragic Generation" appeared first in *The Savoy*. There it included a final paragraph which was deleted in "The Tragic Generation" partly, perhaps, because of a dwindling over the years of the French Symbolist influence over Yeats that was at its height when he wrote the essay. By 1921 he could view his own "decadent period" with detachment, and even appreciate his narrow escape from the dangers it held for him as for others. But the deleted passage indicates that even in the nineties his concept of the divided personality was, at least in its broadest outlines, staked out so far as to include the "daimon"—that vaguely defined other, "buried," self which serves as a guide to spiritual fulfillment:

No matter what he talked of, there was in his voice, in his face, or in his words, something of the "voluminous tenderness" which Mr. Bain has called, I believe, "the basis of all immorality," and of the joyous serenity and untroubled perception of those who commune with spiritual ideas. One felt always that he was a great temperament, the servant of a great daimon, and fancied, as one listened to his vehement sentences that his temperament, his daimon, had been made uncontrollable that he might live the life needful for its perfect expression in art, and yet escape the bonfire.[14]

Yeats must have been aware at the time of his more intimate friends' divided personalities, and even if he could not fully explain the nature of their deficiencies, he was certainly convinced that their search for perfect artistic expression at the cost of ordinary happiness in their lives was the noblest of possible endeavors.

He went still further in the essay, explaining that the ideal world to which Verlaine's uncontrollable daimon would inevitably lead him is not merely a more perfect version of our world, but one which is totally different. It follows that the values of this ideal world which is also the world of art—the Byzantium of later years undoubtedly—must also be totally different. Walter Pater, mentor to the Rhymers' Club, had affirmed the opposition of the artist's morality to that of the ordinary man. The opposition is implicit in Yeats's doctrine of the mask; Dante is a perfect example, and "great temperaments" like Verlaine, in spite of their conventional moral deficiencies, even because of them, may be the real possessors of truth and virtue. "The ideal world," the deleted passage continues, "when it opens its fountains, dissolves by its mysterious excitement in this man sanity, which is but the art of understanding the mechanical world, and in this man morality, which is but the art of living there with comfort; and, seeing this, we grow angry and forget that the Incarnation has none the less need of our reverence because it has taken place in a manger of the dim passions, or bring perhaps our frankincense and myrrh in secret, lest a little truth madden our world."[15] The higher reality of the "ideal world," then, had been affirmed long before Yeats began *The Autobiography,* but the passage deleted from the *Savoy* essay gives no quarter to the vital relationship of the individual mind with the external world, a relationship that he only later found to be important. Besides this, the other conceptual development to come later was that of *Hodos Chameliontos,* which, applied in retrospect to the tragedies of the nineties, gave philosophical meaning to one of the more disturbing and enigmatical periods of his life. The pursuit of reality, or truth, is noble whether or not it is successful; it might even be called heroic, since those men who undertake it often become irretrievably lost in the moral and intellectual wilderness which lies in its path.

In *The Trembling of the Veil,* the portrait of the French Symbolist poet Verlaine indirectly provides a link to Mallarmé's phrase that Yeats had incorporated into his design and used as the title of the book itself. It also underlines the relationship, heightened in Yeats's imagination despite the apparent truth of Graham Hough's statement that the nineties "were a state of mind that originated in France," of the English "decadents" to their generally considered more sophisticated and extravagant French counterparts. In presenting his friends in this light, however, Yeats is being somewhat unfair to them. A glance at their lives and work—the extravagance of which has been commonly exaggerated on both sides—does not really bear out the relationship to the extent he implies; as Hough goes on to say, the Englishmen were "small beer compared with their French counterparts" because they were "translators and adaptors of ideas not their own."[16] There was a very real French influence but, in addition to the fact that while French "decadent" artists had accomplished for the first time the expression of certain genuine insights into universal human experience those in England often expressed little more than mere eccentricity, the Englishmen were not even consistent in their translating and adapting. Wilde, for instance, displayed his best wit at fashionable dinner parties, Johnson turned to religious orthodoxy to satisfy his spiritual needs, and Beardsley's satire interwove his art inextricably with the actual world around him. Dowson probably came closer to the French model, but the English artists of the nineties evinced no desire like Mallarmé's to surround the work of art with a belt in order to isolate it from the physical world. They professed an interest solely in expressing their own emotions, but they lacked the intellectual discipline by which they would have been able to account for the exclusiveness of their interest or relate their emotions to the emotions of others and to the world; the result was the egoistic personal utterance to which J. B. Yeats had always so strongly objected.

Nor can Yeats's friends justly be accused of a decadent sterility, as can perhaps—though with only partial justice—Mallarmé and Rimbaud. Although there were periods when self-absorption stifled the creative impulse, they were on the whole as competent and prolific as their limited talents and the shortness of their careers permitted; Yeats alone produced remarkably little poetry (considering the dimensions of his talent) during the second half of the decade. And if the moral aberrations of the Englishmen's lives are to be regarded as a manifestation of the excessive romantic egoism that makes men indifferent to the world's expectations, hence decadent, these too were very mild compared with those of, say, Verlaine or Rimbaud. But Yeats had formulated his life into an evolving pattern, and his friends of the nineties had a vital role to play in representing its most subjective phases. Their brief lives, only slightly altered and simplified, readily lent themselves to filling out his design.

"The Tragic Generation" concludes with a series of vignettes. Each comprises figures who, for one reason or another, feel alienated from the life around them. In consequence, all agree with the poet Dauthendey[17] in a desire to express their "scorn for reality," that is, the reality of the physical world and society's conventional values. In some, perhaps, this scorn when examined would reveal only eccentricity; in others it would reveal the "elect and chosen souls" who had ventured into the wilderness.

The world having arrived at the breaking point symbolized by phase twenty-two, this generation of artists had witnessed the shift into the primary, objective half of the cycle. The generation was tragic because under the spell of the abstract age in which it had been trapped, it had lost vital contact with the world; it had renounced the visible world and engaged in a desperate search for truth and reality, a search ironically too abstract to end otherwise than in frustration. But the renunciation itself was one which Yeats regarded as natural for the symbolic artist who finds reality in the creative imagination rather than in the physical world, who is compelled like Axël to isolate himself from life, or to destroy his life as a sacrifice to his art. The terrible choice between perfection of the life or of the work became an abiding obsession for Yeats, who was compellingly drawn to both; the fact that fulfillment of one appeared to involve necessarily the destruction of the other constantly pressed upon his mind. To find a way of combining the artist's life, or his withdrawal from life, with the life of the man of action is central to Yeats's search for unity of being.

He discovers that during the nineties his own work as well

as the work of his friends was becoming exaltedly isolated from life: "I am certain that there was something in myself compelling me to attempt creation of an art as separate from everything heterogeneous and casual, from all character and circumstances, as some Herodiade of our theatre, dancing seemingly alone in her narrow moving luminous circle." Mallarmé had himself sought desperately this sublime isolation for his poetry. In the dance, and perhaps in Mallarmé's poetry, the purity of Pater's "condition of music" is almost perfectly realized in the submersion of content into form. The isolated, cold, ferocious innocence of Salome in Mallarmé's "Herodiade" is most vivid in Yeats's mind when he speaks of his own creative impulse during those years, but her devouring passion in Wilde's conception of her, Beardsley's bizarre illustrations one of which Yeats at the time considered his most beautiful work, Moreau's elaborately romantic painting, and the cruel indifference of beauty's enchantment in Symons's "The Dance of the Daughters of Herodias" all combine into an image that Yeats associates with the imminence of lunar phase fifteen, "the moment before revelation" when subjective impulse totally absorbs the individual mind, making life impossible. "When I think of the moment before revelation," he says in *A Vision,* "I think of Salome—she, too, delicately tinted or maybe mahogany dark—dancing before Herod and receiving the Prophet's head in her indifferent hands, and wonder if what seems to us decadence was not in reality the exaltation of the muscular flesh and of civilisation perfectly achieved."[18] This image of the *femme fatale* as dancer combines perfectly the beautiful realization of symbolic reality in the work of art with the destruction of life. And in the ecstatic expression, devoid of all intellectual and moral, that is objective, impulse, is present what may be one of the world's primal images conjured up out of the corporate imagination, since a fascination with an elaborate, all encompassing vision of beauty is in certain ways shared by the elaborate artist with the Aran Islander responding out of an age-old primitive instinct. The Irish Sidhe traveled in the whirling winds that in the Middle Ages were called the dance of the daughters of Herodias.[19]

In their desperate search the artists of the nineties showed themselves capable of the most profound beauty, the omnivorous beauty Yeats identifies with a "tragic joy" deriving from artistic transcendence of temporal experience. "We begin to live," he says, "when we have conceived life as tragedy." Johnson, Dowson, Beardsley and the others were "men who had found life out and were awakening from the dream"; aware that they could not have it both ways, that they had to choose between the search for ordinary happiness and the search for the symbolic reality of art, the perfection of the image coming in Yeats's system only at phase fifteen, they deliberately chose the latter and brought tragedy to their lives. But the tragedy is itself a cause for joy, because in making the choice for art they had at least for the moment reduced the physical reality to insignificance:

> Irrational streams of blood are staining earth;
> Empedocles has thrown all things about;
> Hector is dead and there's a light in Troy;
> We that look on but laugh in tragic joy.

All tragic heroes, Yeats says in "Lapis Lazuli," "know that Hamlet and Lear are gay;/Gaiety transfiguring all that dread." The carved Chinamen upon reaching the half-way house high on the mountain,

> On all the tragic scene they stare.
> One asks for mournful melodies;
> Accomplished fingers begin to play.
> Their eyes mid many wrinkles, their eyes,
> Their ancient, glittering eyes, are gay.[20]

Yeats's celebration of his friends transfigures them from a group of gifted men who had led pathetic lives into what he calls "the tragic generation." The epithet is not one of simple sentiment, for if he is unfair to the mere facts of their lives, in being so he endows them with lives exalted in the gaiety of tragedy.

In the objective world taking form toward the end of the nineteenth century, however, only comedy was possible, a comedy which, next to the "subtle colour and nervous rhythm" of the tragic generation's hesitating, subjective genius, was harsh, confident, and barbarous. "The Savage God" identified with the age of comedy, and to Yeats's mind celebrated in Alfred Jarry's grotesque play *Ubu Roi*, recalls the "growing murderousness of the world" foreseen toward the end of "Four Years," and the first stirrings of the antichrist in "The Second Coming." From the perspective of 1921, after the advent of Wyndham Lewis, of the Imagists, of Ezra Pound's formless style "interrupted, broken, twisted into nothing by its . . . nervous obsession, nightmare, stammering confusion," and of T. S. Eliot's "grey, cold, dry" art,[21] and after the first World War, the terror of the Black and Tans, and the Irish Civil War, the art and lives of the tragic generation ("the last romantics" as he more tenderly refers to them elsewhere) must have appeared more than ever made of a substance too rare to exist in what was becoming increasingly an objective, dehumanized, and hostile world.

The tragedy of the nineties was not complete until the first years of the new century: Beardsley died in 1898, Wilde and Dowson in 1900, Johnson in 1902, Henley in 1903, and Davidson in 1909. Yet, as early as 1896 the Rhymers' Club had already been disbanded for two years,[22] and *The Savoy*, typical of the generation in which it had flourished, expired in its youth. In "The Stirring of the Bones" Yeats places the end of the era at 1897. In spite of his sadness at its passing, he describes his response to the onset of the objective half of the cycle as enthusiastic. He found it refreshing to be thrust back into the commonplace of worldly affairs after having already accompanied his friends further along their holy passage than seemed wise. Viewing objective experience as antithetical to his nature, he says he deliberately sought it as a means to union with his anti-self. But the unity achieved through deliberately chosen experience, he later came to understand, can only be piecemeal, of the isolated moment or event, whereas true unity of being is found emotionally and instinctively.

Despite an impression to the contrary given by the arrangement of material in *The Trembling of the Veil*, Yeats's nationalist activity was pursued continuously throughout the nineties, though between 1894 and 1897 almost entirely from London and through literary means. The clear delineation of life patterns was only formulated in his mind with anything approaching artistic or philosophical detachment years after the events, and after he had discovered a philosophy that could give them meaning. During his actual involvement in the Irish affairs of the nineties even his motives were much less abstruse than they appear in either "Ireland After Parnell" or "The Stirring of the Bones." His deep-rooted national feeling was certainly an important factor in the role he played, but his most immediate reason for throwing himself so completely into Irish politics was to advance his love affair with Maud Gonne. Although he always maintained an independent point of view, often directly opposing hers, his sense of values was strained many times to please or influence her. He is more candid about this in "Memoirs," where he describes his plans to return from England to Ireland and begin a new movement:

During my years in London I had come to think of societies and movements to encourage literature, and create it where it was not, as absurd—is not the artist always solitary, and yet now I wished to form societies and to influence men perhaps. I began to justify this plan to this nervous mocking self by saying that Ireland which could not support a critical press must find a substitute. A moment later that nervous self would convict me of insincerity and show me that I was seeking a field of work that would not be demoralizing, as I thought that even the most necessary politics were, not for all, but mostly for her, whose soul I partly judged from her physical beauty and partly knew to be distinguished and subtle.[23]

Yeats had managed to divert Maud Gonne's interest temporarily to the intellectual side of the movement he describes in "Ireland After Parnell" so that she might live a life consistent with her beauty and character. But she soon left it for what was to her more exciting, a life of activist political revolution, which, moreover, would yield more immediate practical results.[24] It was now her turn to divert him to those "demoralizing" political activities that he describes in "Memoirs" as wasteful and none of his business. Yet, he reasons in "The Stirring of the Bones," just in so far as they were not his business, he was allured by them as a means of finding his anti-self. On this reasoning he constructs a vantage point from which to view his political activity at this time.

His nationalist interest now shifted from the organization of literary societies and a preoccupation with the soul of the race into the center of practical political action. This action, notwithstanding his desire to create unity, ended by furthering those nationalist abstractions which had already contributed to the hostile division of Ireland and to his own alienation from a life he found attractive and meaningful. Acting merely out of abstract principle himself, the little success he had in his effort to unite Ireland's divided factions was superficial, isolated, and in no way resembling the unity of culture he sought for Ireland, or the unity of being he sought for himself. In the course of his occult experiments of several years before, he was often deluded into thinking he had discovered a significant image only to find it later transformed or vanished entirely; now, believing he had created a form of national unity or had obtained Maud Gonne's support on an issue, he invariably found that there were new causes for argument or that she had completely distorted his ideas.

Yeats sees Maud Gonne herself moving with a vitality so dynamic that it made his own activities seem sedentary. And where he had been thoughtful and calculating, she was super-stitious, acting, as he thought, out of a power beyond her own mind, a power emanating from her beauty that "suggested joy and freedom" while appealing, through an association with ancient images of mythical Irish queens, to the imagina-tion of the race. With this instinctive, perhaps "daimonically" inspired power, she was able to achieve a measure of national unity impossible for Yeats with his deliberate intellectual effort.

For all this mystic power, the unity she achieved proved to be superficial. During the Queen Victoria Jubilee riot in Dublin, the crowd was magnetized as if it were a single person by Maud Gonne's will. But after the victory, which morally was real enough, there was no national feeling of gratifica-tion as there certainly would have been with the achievement of real unity of mind and purpose. There was instead only remorse of conscience, vows of hatred, the old factiousness, patriotic buffoonery, and a general state of organizational shoddiness and pathetic devotion to a confused and divided cause.

Maud Gonne's power, residing in her beauty, had tri-umphed. But "beauty," Yeats says, "is from the antithetical self," and she could not make "the denial or the dissolution of the [primary] self"[25] that the subjective individual makes while pursuing the mask; she rejected her beauty and tried to find strength in objective action. Temporarily inspired into an antithetical state of mind on the edge of unity of being in which she could have achieved great things, her nature eventually drove her into union with her body of fate rather than with her mask, and her power was reduced to the objective mediocrity of Irish politics.

In *The Trembling of the Veil* Yeats first describes his friends' attempts to forge fullness of being out of their fragmented lives. Then he describes his own attempts to achieve unity, first by finding it for Ireland, and then by eliciting images from the great memory through the sheer strength of his will. Seeking unity with an abstract deliberateness characteristic of his age, and vesting almost total authority in his own subjective impulses while rejecting that of the external world, he was for a time condemned with the rest of his generation to the confusion of *Hodos Chameliontos*. His subsequent grasping after objective experience as a means to union with his anti-self failed because of the deliberateness which characterized this effort as it had the previous one.

Notwithstanding all these frustrations, he describes a series of events beginning as early as 1896 in which, he says, he had begun to find his way off *Hodos Chameliontos*. "Megarithma," "a certain symbolic personality," had advised him to "live near water and avoid woods 'because they concentrate the solar ray.' "[26] This advice was supervened during the following summer by a vision at Tullira Castle, Edward Martyn's home in County Galway. Here, Yeats's invocations of the moon, performed as in his early experiments by meditation and the use of symbol, again raised images complemented by those in the visions of others.[27] Yeats learned on this occasion, however, that the woman shooting an arrow into the sky, the centaur, and the star, all of which appeared in his vision, were not only related to images in the children's and in Arthur Symons's visions and in Fiona Macleod's story, and to "Megarithma's" advice as well,[28] but that they were ancient cabalistic symbols of which he could have had no earthly knowledge. They were, he speculates, a glimpse of "some great event taken place in some world where myth is reality," or of something "in the memory of the race . . . believed thousands of years ago,"[29] and he had called them up from the great memory. The old enigma of their meaning, however, remained; Yeats was able to learn (from the London coroner and cabalist Dr. W. Wynn Westcott, according to "Memoirs") of certain symbolic correspondences, but more than this would not come except through revelation.

The "invisible gates" finally appeared to be opening while he was at Coole. Having temporarily given up his struggle for unity, he had begun to spend his summers there, comfortably submitting himself to Lady Gregory's solicitous authority in an effort to regain his strength and peace of mind. Both were lost on *Hodos Chameliontos* he concludes in "The Stirring of the Bones," but they were undoubtedly also much dissipated by the frustrations of his love affair with Maud Gonne and by a lung ailment which may have been tuberculosis.[30] Yeats's friendship with Lady Gregory, he implies, had itself been foreseen in some vague way in his spiritual experiences. He is explicit in "Memoirs," saying that at moments he had "believed or half believed—we cannot judge the power of those shadows—that she came in reply to these evocations for are not the common people and their wisdom under the moon, and her house is at the edge of [a] lake"; but he could find no explanation of the warning to "avoid woods." The idea that his friendship with Lady Gregory was initiated through preternatural intervention remains an unspoken implication in "The Stirring of the Bones," where Yeats concentrates on bringing his major theme to a climax. At Coole, he says, "the first few simple thoughts that now, grown complex through their contact with other thoughts, explain the world, came to me from beyond my own mind."[31] The mental and physical collapse which he attributes to

Hodos Chameliontos, it appears, was related directly to the raising of his mind to that highest pitch necessary for revelation.

Those "first few simple thoughts" were in fact embedded in Yeats's mind over a year earlier, as the Verlaine essay testifies, and indeed as his first coming alive to the possibilities of the *Anima Mundi* signifies; but it was more consonant with his total outlook, and consistent with the supposedly preternatural origins of *A Vision* itself, that the philosophy which was already an inchoate part of his mental frame of reference appear whole in a visionary glimpse through the opening "invisible gates." He is careful to stress the absence of deliberate effort in producing the phenomenon, since penetration to the invisible world comes when one is immersed in this one. While he gives us to understand that this penetration was an intensely emotional experience, his account of it does not convey the sense of trauma he has led us to expect. During a period of time when he was generally distracted with political matters, and just at a moment when his mind was deeply engrossed in pagan rather than Christian thoughts, Yeats says, he felt a powerful sense of Christian devotion. This incongruous and uncharacteristic feeling was followed shortly afterward by a voice speaking of God's need for every man's soul, and later by the first vision of a series that was ultimately to reveal the concept of the mask—which is central in his philosophical system as he later developed it. Yeats's expectations had thus been realized. Philosophy had come through revelation, not when he was deliberately seeking it, but when the "invisible gates" were opened; it had come likewise when they were opened for Blake, Swedenborg, and Boehme. Yeats had at last obtained a clear glimpse into the *Anima Mundi.*

With his vision finally quivering into focus, Yeats was able to embark eagerly and optimistically upon a new phase of his life (". . . in 1897 a new scene was set, new actors appeared").

The veil of the Temple, a metaphor equivalent to the "invisible gates" but eliciting greater implications of sanctity, had previously concealed life's inner reality. It was now beginning to tremble into motion, ultimately, he hoped, to be rent apart. Having posited a vision of reality as a foundation, he could better order and give meaning to his life and thereby to his national feeling and his art. Thought and emotion might now move toward unity.

Tracing the pattern of his life in *Reveries* and *The Trembling of the Veil* according to its passage through the lunar cycle, as Yeats himself almost certainly did, we might find it beginning in a typically primary, objective, state, but passing through the phases of lessening primary impulse as his personality expanded along with the diversification of his interests. Then, as he began to achieve independence of opinion and artistic expression, he moved into the antithetical, subjective, half of the cycle. Nearing the subjective meridian at phase fifteen, he was partially (but, it must be emphasized, only partially) absorbed along with his friends of the nineties into a virtual narcissistic fixation resulting in his loss of meaningful communion with the external world, and in his sojourn upon *Hodos Chameliontos*. In 1897, as if suddenly jolted into an awareness of what was happening to him, he was impelled forward in what appears a single impulse to phase twenty-two, where Western civilization had itself arrived in the historical cycle, and where the cycle breaks again into the objective phases. For a brief moment now, Yeats lived in apparent harmony with his age. But having been endowed with a basically subjective nature, this harmony was not congenial to him. He moved with his series of discoveries at Coole back into phase seventeen where he was essentially to remain, and where, subjective strength being dominant but held in check by a constant objective pressure, unity of being was most possible.[32]

six

CULTURE AS
RECONCILIATION

Yeats completed *Dramatis Personae* thirteen years after *The Trembling of the Veil*. Although actually completing the earlier work's overall design, he gives the new section of his autobiography a somewhat different perspective, which is accentuated by the passage of time and by the complication of additional motives. Yeats began writing the book shortly after Lady Gregory's death, intending it to be a memoir of her, but it quickly grew into an account of the beginnings of the Irish Literary Theatre which they had founded together. Notwithstanding the alteration of the title from his intended *Lady Gregory* to *Dramatis Personae*, the theater's history becomes largely a vehicle for the further exploration of personality and culture, and Lady Gregory remains the book's heroine. George Moore, who along with Edward Martyn was also a principal figure in the early days of the theater, is the antagonist. It is partly the juxtaposition of his character and Martyn's with Lady Gregory's that makes more poignant her image as one of Yeats's "beautiful lofty things."

George Moore is so good a foil because Yeats is strongly impelled to surpass his *Hail and Farewell* in positing an authoritative history of the movement, and to show that Moore was blind to its practicalities and ideals. He also wanted to show that Moore's portraits of Lady Gregory and himself were unrealistic as well as malicious. Although Moore's statements mixed blame with praise (in the end he did credit Yeats with the success of the Irish literary revival) they were suffused with a note of mockery which became more offensive to Yeats the longer he reflected upon it. In *Ave,* the first volume, for example, Moore describes Yeats as "lank as a rook, a-dream in black silhouette on a flowered wall-paper."* [1] A few pages later comes a still more painfully detailed description of him at the theater, this time as an Irish caricature of a Bohemian: "When I saw him he was on exhibition, striding to and forth at the back of the dress circle, a long black cloak drooping from his shoulders, a soft black sombrero on his head, a voluminous black silk tie flowing from his collar, loose black trousers dragging untidily over his long, heavy feet—a man of such excessive appearance that I could not do otherwise . . . than to mistake him for an Irish parody of the poetry that I had seen all my life strutting its rhythmic way in the alleys of the Luxembourg Gardens, preening its rhymes by the fountains, excessive in habit and gait."[2] Elsewhere he mingles professions of admiration with comments that characterize Yeats as vain, pompous, distracted, or importunate. In general, Moore saw Yeats as unobservant, alive only to metaphysical reality.

But his mockery extends to areas other than Yeats's appear-

---

* Quotations from *Hail and Farewell,* by George Moore, are reprinted with permission of Appleton-Century, affiliate of Meredith Press (copyright 1911 by D. Appleton and Company; copyright 1939 by Charles Douglas Medley) and with permission of J. C. Medley and R. G. Medley, owners of the copyright.

ance and outward personality, and in which Yeats was also
sensitive. He describes his speech as picturesque, and compares it to a coach wheel that spins smoothly and easily when
raised from the ground, because it has nothing to turn. He
praises his conversation, but then undercuts the compliment
by saying that "Yeats is thinner in his writings than in his
talk," and that he lacks interest in all the arts except literature.[3] Yeats, moreover, could not have enjoyed Moore's
mockery of his occult interests, although he was accustomed
to abuse on this account. And the image of him as incom-
petent and childishly idealistic in his management of rehear-
sals during the first weeks of the theater must have been
equally distasteful. Most of all, Yeats must have been enraged
when Moore, reflecting on his rejection of Martyn's play
"The Tale of the Town," suggested that abstract thinking
had killed human sympathy in him, that "the metaphysician
. . . has absorbed the human being," that he "was a sort of
monk of literature" and that his intellect had outlived his
heart.[4] Yeats, on the contrary, was preoccupied during much
of his life in uniting the intellect and the heart, something he
felt Moore himself distinctly did not do.

In *Vale,* the final volume of *Hail and Farewell,* Moore
accused Yeats of attacking the middle classes to which his
own family belonged. The accusation, Yeats says in his diary,
was a distortion of a speech appealing to the aristocracy to
support Hugh Lane's projected art gallery.[5] It had at the time
motivated him to write *Reveries Over Childhood and Youth*
as "some sort of an 'apologia' for the Yeats family," and the
prologue and epilogue of *Responsibilities.* But he had as yet
written nothing openly of Moore himself, though the desire
to do so had occupied a corner of his mind for several years.[6]
Reveries had answered the accusation, but without mention-
ing Moore. Now, with Moore dead, Yeats felt free to reply
more directly, and in the salty manner of his mature years.

The study of character in *Dramatis Personae,* then, is not like the abstruse and esoteric distinctions of *The Trembling of the Veil.* It is worldly, personal, indiscreet. Nevertheless, the images Yeats gives his friends are often clarified by reference to the lunar phases of *A Vision* in which he had placed them. Unity of being and unity of culture remain as before, normative. Whereas in *The Trembling of the Veil* Yeats had ultimately penetrated the hidden reality which gave him access to unity of being, the later books of *The Autobiography* complete the design by bringing him to a confrontation with unity of culture, not in Ireland unfortunately, but in Sweden. The fact that this confrontation, unlike the first, took place in the natural world rather than some ideal one reflects the ambivalent contrary pulls for Yeats of the visible and invisible, temporal and spiritual worlds which pervade his thought. This worldly confrontation is itself consistent with the shift toward tangibility in his autobiographical perspective, and is underlined by the documentation of letters and diaries. In the later books Yeats uses his system less overtly and more to understand what he sees than to evolve the invisible world, though that is always there behind the arras.

His conception of the antinomies of self and anti-self is therefore still involved, but the relatively uncomplicated form in which it appears in the "Anima Hominis" section of *Per Amica Silentia Lunae* (the first section of the work, dealing with the temporal world in contrast to the second section, "Anima Mundi," dealing with the spiritual one) is often more helpful than the more fully developed and complex system of *A Vision.* The bifurcation of Lady Gregory's mind, and its consequent effect on her personality illustrate this conception in its best sense. But the antithesis may also occur wherein the results are decidedly less admirable. Opposite natures come together in the personality of Edward Martyn whose "father's family was old and honoured" but whose mother was "but one generation from the peasant." In Martyn they came together for mutual destruction: Yeats believed that the "two traditions met and destroyed each other in his blood, creating the sterility of a mule."[7] Lady Gregory and Martyn furnish Yeats from the beginning with an opposition of personalities.

He sets up this opposition first through a comparison of their houses. Martyn's Tullira Castle betrayed an insincerity and pretentiousness which were the consequences of a misguided attempt to satisfy the tastes of others. No sense of history or tradition enlivened the house. Nearly everything in it was hated by its owner, but hated with a kind of relish because it fed a hatred of life itself, the result of his having substituted abstract principle for living experience.[8] While Martyn appreciated good art for its beauty, he delighted in all that displayed the most distasteful and sordid aspects of life.

Yeats's impression of Coole, Lady Gregory's estate, is much different. Among his most fond and vivid memories is the demesne—the shaded drive, the woods and lake. The pleasure he derived from Coole Park where he spent much of his leisure time belies Moore's repeated remarks in *Hail and Farewell* that he was indifferent to natural beauty.[9] Coole House itself had an architecture which was undistinguished, but in contrast with Tullira, it took its character from the generations of people who had lived in it. Each had left behind objects and made changes that fixed the stamp of his life and personality upon the house, and their accumulation made the house alive. Lady Gregory, unlike Martyn, loved her house, and loved it more as it grew more rich in human associations; even most of the pictures on the walls were painted by artists associated personally with the Gregorys and with Coole.[10] She became preoccupied with the tradition of the house just as Yeats did with the folk tradition of the surrounding countryside to which she had introduced him.

It is by absorbing a sense of tradition and culture, Yeats asserts, rather than by acquiring ordinary intellectual confidence that one attains personal charm and distinction, and even a really profound intellectual capacity. "Culture," he had said, "is the sanctity of the intellect,"[11] and he writes in *Estrangement:* "Is not all charm inherited, whether of the intellect, of the manners, of the character, or of literature? A great lady is as simple as a good poet. Neither possesses anything that is not ancient and their own, and both are full of uncertainty about everything but themselves, about everything that can be changed, about all that they merely think. They assume convictions as if they were a fashion in clothes and remould all slightly."[12] Pleased with the likeness, he returns to the subject several pages later: "Every day I notice some new analogy between the long-established life of the well-born and the artists' life. We come from the permanent things and create them, and instead of old blood we have old emotions and we carry in our heads always that form of society aristocracies create now and again for some brief moment at Urbino or Versailles."[13] At Coole Yeats found "the long-established life of the well-born and the artists' life" joined in their natural, mutual affinity.

The people who had inhabited the house before Lady Gregory were, of course, not her ancestors but her husband's. She was a Persse whose family home was Roxborough. It is well to consider Yeats's description of her family against the background of George Moore's in *Vale*. Says Moore:

> Lady Gregory is a Persse, and the Persses are an ancient Galway family; the best-known branch is Moyaude, for it was at Moyaude that Burton Persse bred and hunted the Galway Blazers for over thirty years . . . till his death. Moyaude has passed away, but Rox-

borough continues, never having indulged in either horses or hounds, a worthy but undistinguished family in love, in war, or in politics, never having indulged in anything except a taste for Bible reading in the cottages. A staunch Protestant family, if nothing else, the Roxborough Persses certainly are. Mrs. Persse and her two elder daughters were ardent soul-gatherers in the days gone by but Lady Gregory did not join them in their missionary work, holding always to the belief that there was great danger in persuading anyone to leave the religion learnt in childhood, for we could never be sure that another would find a place in the heart. In saying as much she wins our hearts, but our intelligence warns us against the seduction, and we remember that we may not acquiesce in what we believe to be error. The ignorant and numbed mind cannot be acceptable to God, so do we think, and take our stand with Mrs. Persse and the elder sisters.[14]

The contrast between this and Yeats's description is emphatic:

She was a type that only the superficial observer could identify with Victorian earnestness, for her point of view was founded, not on any narrow modern habit but upon her sense of great literature, upon her own strange feudal, almost medieval youth. She was a Persse—a form of the name Shakespeare calls Percy—descended from some Duke of Northumberland; her family had settled in the seventeenth century somewhere in the midlands, but finding, the legend declares, the visits of Lord Clanricarde, going and returning between his estate and Dublin, expensive, they had moved that they might be no longer near the high road and bought vast tracts of Galway land . . . The Persses had been soldiers, farmers, riders to hounds and, in the time of the Irish Parliament, politicians; a bridge within the wall commemorated the victory of the Irish Volunteers in 1782, but all had lacked intellectual curiosity until the downfall of their class had all but come.[15]

Moore maintains that the Persses' greatest claim to distinction rests in their ancestors' breeding of fine horses; Yeats finds that they possibly are descended from an ancient noble family immortalized by Shakespeare, that their hospitality was sought by other noble families of high rank, and that they were distinguished soldiers, farmers, sportsmen, and patriots. Their aristocratic distinction is magnified, moreover, by Yeats's insouciant tone and by his implication that their honorable roles were pure instinct, uncorrupted by intellectual contrivance.

Contrasting even more strikingly with Moore's, Yeats's account describes the Persses during the time of Lady Gregory's girlhood, her immediate family being the object of Moore's most conspicuous abuse:

> Popular legend attributes to all the sons of the house daring and physical strength; some years ago, Free State Ministers were fond of recounting the adventures of Lady Gregory's "Seven Brothers" who, no matter who objected to their rents, or coveted their possessions, were safe "because had one been killed, the others would have run down and shot the assassin"; how the wildest of the brothers, excluded by some misdemeanour from a Hunt Ball, had turned a hose on the guests; how, a famous shot, he had walked into a public-house in a time of disturbance and put a bullet through every number on the clock. They had all the necessities of life on the mountain, or within the walls of their demesne, exporting great quantities of game, ruling their tenants, as had their fathers before, with a despotic benevolence, were admired, and perhaps loved, for the Irish people, however lawless, respect a rule founded upon some visible supremacy.[16]

Legend serves as historical authority for both Moore and Yeats, though only Yeats acknowledges it. Both men accept this authority, but each selects and colors it in a way that satisfies his own inclination. Moore must certainly have known of Lady Gregory's "Seven Brothers." For Yeats they were "figures from the eighteenth century," the century of the Irish Renaissance as he thought, which had produced many of the Anglo-Irish heroes with whom he took pride in identifying himself.[17] Whether the brothers were in fact the attractively flamboyant figures he portrays or whether they were admired and loved by their tenants is of no matter here; his account of them recalls his own abiding fascination with the "wasteful virtues" of passionate men, and counters Moore's allegations that the family was "undistinguished . . . never having indulged in anything except a taste for Bible reading in the cottages," "a staunch Protestant family, if nothing else." The effect of Yeats's elaborate apologia for the Persses is to give Lady Gregory herself a past worthy of her husband and of Coole. If real culture is largely dependent upon tradition and the kinship of noble spirits, the hostess at Coole was an aristocrat in her own right and felicitous in her position. Even when Yeats speaks of the Persses' "proselytism," his pardoning it as a misguided expression of love suggests gentle disapproval, or perhaps a straining of his own sensibilities to minimize the offense. In contrast, Moore's approval smacks of satire and ridicule. Later in the same chapter of *Vale* Moore speaks of "the whining voice of the proselytizer" in reference to Lady Gregory herself (though he, rather unconvincingly, puts the words into Martyn's mouth).[18] Yeats flatly declares that Lady Gregory, "the born student of the great literature of the world [Moore boasts of having read as little as possible] cannot proselytize."[19]

The contrasting images of Lady Gregory and George Moore point up the differences rather than the relatively superficial similarities in their backgrounds. Both were descended from landed families in the west of Ireland, and both had traveled extensively abroad—Moore deliberately to absorb Continental culture and Lady Gregory to accompany her husband in the diplomatic service. The effect of this experience upon Lady Gregory, Yeats says, had been to add to a natural compassion and psychological perception already enriched by great literature, a deep insight into her own country, into its "permanent relationships, associations," and a sense of the responsibility placed upon her by "her station and her character."[20] Yeats concedes to Moore a knowledge of modern drama and of Impressionist painting which might be attributed to his stay abroad, but he believed him always to be, beneath the sophisticated surface, a typical, though corrupted peasant.

In *Dramatis Personae* Yeats is bent on setting right the record of events that Moore had described in *Hail and Farewell*. His first meeting with Moore and the beginning of his friendship with Synge, Moore's artistic associations in Paris, the honorary dinner given by T. P. Gill, the reworking of Martyn's "The Tale of the Town," and like events take on decidedly contrasting accents in the two books, with Yeats generally trying to restore the dignity to individuals and events that Moore's derision had taken away, and to expose Moore's fatuousness where he had pictured himself cultured and worldly.

At the same time, Yeats is careful not to take Martyn's view that Moore "has no good points."[21] In the 1901 volume of *Samhain*, written shortly before their break, he had praised Moore's contribution to the establishment of the Irish Literary Theatre, doubting "if it could have been done at all without his knowledge of the stage."[22] In *Dramatis Personae* he grants him an extraordinary capacity for dramatic construction, an instinct for effective prosaic language (which, however, arose out of his lack of feeling for words), and the achievement of having created five realistic novels which were artistic masterpieces of their kind. Moreover, in conceding Moore's wit, a capacity for remorse, a captivating if at times exasperating naivety in company with his brutality and Continental air of *tout comprendre,* and even a willingness, surprising in view of his vanity, to retreat on occasion from public attention, Yeats accords Moore the bifurcated nature of the artist. The concession is an important one, since Yeats disapproved of Moore's literary realism as well as of his personal behavior, and it greatly qualifies the derisive image of Moore that Yeats mainly displays. Moore had gone out of his way to make a show of doing Yeats justice and Yeats was no less gracious.

But in the end, Yeats's image of Moore is less complimentary than Moore's of him.

Even at this, Yeats had toned down the image in *Dramatis Personae* from a still harsher one painted in his diary in 1913:

Moore . . . is the born demagogue and in nothing more than in his love of the wealth. He has always a passion for some crowd, is always deliberately inciting them against somebody. He shares the mob's materialism and the mob's hatred of any privilege, which is an incommunicable gift. He can imagine himself rich, he cannot imagine himself with fine manners, and the mere thought of such manners gives him a longing to insult somebody. He looks at style or the pursuit of it, in the same way. On the other hand he has the demagogic virtues, which are all bound up with logic. When logic is master, and his personality is for the moment quiet, he has intellectual honesty and courage. These impersonal moods alternate with orgies of personal vanity during which he sees all the closed doors of the world, and bangs them with his fist and shrieks at the windows. If his vanity had not made self possession impossible, substituting a desire to startle, and to shock for the solitude, the first laborious creation of genius, he might have been a great writer, or at any rate as great a writer as a man of wholly external vision can be. That antithesis which I see in all artists between the artistic and the daily self was in his case too crude and simple and the daily part too powerful, and his ignorance, and ignorance often helps external vision, deprived him of all discipline.

The conclusion is essentially the same as in *Dramatis Personae,* but the characterization is given in blunter terms. It was impossible, Yeats suggests, for Moore to have become a great artist, since the elements of conflict within him were too crudely divided to be brought into harmony. When he tried to reconcile his inclination for the vainglorious display of himself or his abilities with the disciplined restraint needed for artistic achievement, he only became entangled in mental and emotional complexities, in a conflict between an objective, intellectual association with external events, an association based on logic that eliminates the personality (this association being appropriate to his talent), and an egocentric, emotional involvement in them that is all personality. In terms of *A Vision* Moore shares with Shaw the worldly advantages of phase twenty-one, but his entanglement is a consequence of his being "out of phase," whereby "he will parade an imaginary naïveté, even blunder in his work, encourage in himself stupidities of spite or sentiment, or commit calculated indiscretions simulating impulse."[23] "He was all self and yet had so little self that he would destroy his reputation, or that of some friend" in an effort to call attention to the image of himself he was conscientiously trying to create.[24]

Yeats finds that it was in the attempt to create this image of himself that Moore pursued literary style with such disastrous results. His pursuit of style, unlike Douglas Hyde's spontaneous, or even Yeats's own slow and painful discovery of a fresh "living speech," was carried on by imitation and by the deliberate exaggeration of what he believed style to be. Seeking an image so deliberately, whether in a literary style foreign to his personality or in personal eccentricity, led Moore to *Hodos Chameliontos*. In the more worldly context of *Dramatis Personae*, Moore's collaboration with Yeats on *Diarmuid and Grania* had "set him upon a pursuit of style that made barren his later years."[25] And his personal eccentricities, whether manifested in acts of brutality, of which there were many, or of kindness, of which there were also many, or even acts of innocuous vanity along with the myth-making which served this vanity, earned him enemies everywhere.

His greatest enemy, it would seem, and at the same time his closest friend, was Martyn. Martyn and Moore were always at odds with each other, and yet because of their opposite natures they completed each other's personalities. Yeats had used them earlier as models for the holy man and his lecherous friend described in *The Cat and the Moon*,[26] and he now counterposes them as a smaller opposition than that between themselves and Lady Gregory. Both, he says, suffered in their heritage from the shortcomings that made Irish-Catholic civilization the antithesis of the more refined and sophisticated Protestant culture exemplified in its best form by the traditions of Coole. He had described the antithesis in his diary in 1913 emphasizing the destructive role of Catholic women, probably with Moore's treatment of Lady Gregory's family in mind:

I have been told that the crudity common to all the Moores came from the mother's family—Mayo squireens probably half peasants in education and occupation—for his father was a man of education and power and old descent. His mother's blood seems to have affected him and his brother, as the peasant strain has affected Edward Martyn. There has been a union of incompatibles and consequent sterility. In Martyn too one finds an intellect, which should have given creative power, but in Martyn the sterility is complete, though unlike Moore he has self possession and taste. He only fails in words. It is as though he had been put into the wrong body. Both men are examples of the way Irish civilization is held back by the lack of education of Irish Catholic women. An Irish Catholic will not marry a Protestant, and hitherto the women have checked again and again the rise into some world of refinement of Catholic households. The whole system of Irish Catholicism, pulling down the able and well born if it pulls up the peasant as I think it does. [*sic*] A long continuity of culture like that at Coole could not have arisen in a single Catholic family in Ireland since the Middle Ages.

In *Dramatis Personae* his sectarian outlook is less distinct: he recognizes a growing number of enlightened Irish Catholics, and the pronounced cultural inferiority of Catholic to Protestant Ireland suggested in the diary appears considerably diminished. Martyn's "religion," he says, "was a peasant religion; he knew nothing of those interpretations, casuistries, whereby my Catholic acquaintances adapt their ancient rules to modern necessities."[27] The support of *The Countess Cath-*

leen by Father Finlay and Father Barry draws into focus that element of Catholic Ireland which had succeeded in transcending Martyn's "peasant religion," but Yeats remains conscious of the disproportionately large number of Irish Protestant leaders and heroes, and of the fact that the Protestant community included most of educated and cultured Ireland.[28] Yet, if the aristocratic qualities of Coole (which, unlike Tullira, had not been dominated by an uneducated woman, like Martyn's mother, pulling down standards of taste) were essentially limited to Protestant Ireland, he was nonetheless anxious that they be spread throughout the nation. If this could be accomplished, Ireland would attain unity by combining Protestant culture, taste, and learning with a capacity for strong emotions lacking in Protestant Ireland but predominant among Irish Catholics.

Yeats sees this unity, meanwhile, imaged in Lady Gregory. In her the character of a great lady found expression in the Kiltartan peasant imagination and dialect. Unlike Moore, she expressed not her ordinary self or what she might have egoistically pictured herself to be, but her opposite, in this resembling John Synge, "a sick man picturing energy, a doomed man picturing gaiety," and Yeats himself who "ruffled in a manly pose/For all his timid heart."[29] In *Per Amica Silentia Lunae* Yeats had spoken of her capacity to write out of her anti-self: "I have sometimes told one close friend that her only fault is a habit of harsh judgment with those who have not her sympathy, and she has written comedies where the wickedest people seem but bold children. She does not know why she has created that world where no one is ever judged, a high celebration of indulgence, but to me it seems that her ideal of beauty is the compensating dream of a nature wearied out by over-much judgment."[30] The trait is typical of Lady Gregory's phase (twenty-four) in *A Vision*: "There may be great intolerance for all who break or resist the code, and great tolerance for all the evil of the world that is clearly beyond it whether above it or below." It was in the beauty of her "compensating dream" that Lady Gregory had her vision of the world in which she found expression: "Lady Gregory, in her life much artifice, in her nature much pride, was born to see the glory of the world in a peasant mirror."[31] She had succeeded in achieving literary style, and the ingredients that had united to give it to her also united to give her personality. Because this personality came in a form so totally identified with Ireland, because she united in herself the tradition, taste, wisdom, and charm of the true aristocrat, with a capacity to seem one among the common people, she created at Coole an image of the unity of culture Yeats was seeking on a national scale. With *The Bounty of Sweden* (written ten years earlier) in mind, Yeats prefigures in this image the unity of culture he was to discover in Sweden, and thereby the Swedish-style Utopia he envisioned for Ireland.

Dramatis Personae brought Yeats's autobiography only to the year 1902, although it was not until 1923 that he visited Sweden. It is likely that he originally intended to fill the twenty-one year gap, but he died scarcely more than three years after completing *Dramatis Personae* and wrote nothing new of a directly autobiographical nature during that time. The collections of notes from his 1909 diary, however, already published separately in 1926 and 1928 as *Estrangement* and *The Death of Synge,* give some account of his thoughts between the two periods of his life. Following upon *Dramatis Personae,* they have the interest of Yeats's candid reflections on many subjects, and lend structural balance to *The Autobiography.* They bear a relation to *Dramatis Personae* similar to that of "Ireland After Parnell" to "Four Years," the pattern in both instances involving a movement from Yeats's concern with individuals to a comprehensive image of Ireland.

Estrangement and *The Death of Synge* are also closely linked in several other ways, most obviously by their proximity and likeness of method. Yeats begins *Estrangement* by justifying its casual, disconnected form: "To keep these notes natural and useful to me," he says, "I must keep one note from leading on to another, that I may not surrender myself to literature. Every note must come as a casual thought, then it will be my life. Neither Christ nor Buddha nor Socrates wrote a book, for to do that is to exchange life for a logical process."[32] In *The Death of Synge* he finds the value of his journal entries primarily therapeutic: "These notes are morbid, but I heard a man of science say that all progress is at the outset pathological, and I write for my own good."[33] Both statements as they originally stand in the diary serve for his own guidance, but within the context of *The Autobiography* they have the effect of disarming criticism which might turn on the apparent formlessness of the books.

These books also have a precise function in presenting Yeats's theme, his confrontation of unity of culture. By intensifying the contrast between national images, they set the ground for his representation of Sweden as a civilization that had all but eliminated the emotional and intellectual shortcomings which continued to stifle Ireland's progress in becoming a cultivated nation. *Estrangement* expresses Yeats's sense of being alienated from popular Irish attitudes, from the factiousness and ignorance that he believed stood in the way of unity of culture during those years, and discovers by a different method and in different circumstances what had already been discovered in "The Tragic Generation"—the potential destructiveness for the artist of conventional values and popular movements. "The Tragic Generation," however, focuses on the tragedies of the artists, and on the recondite implications of those tragedies, whereas *Estrangement* focuses on the more worldly shortcomings of the society which was largely responsible for them. Yeats believed that the Irish attitudes that caused his own estrangement also in large measure caused Synge's death.

John Synge appears earlier in *The Autobiography*, beginning to emerge into prominence in *Estrangement*, but he never appears in so direct a light as O'Leary, Johnson, Lady Gregory, and some others. In *The Death of Synge* Yeats places him clearly before us for the first time, though his personality is as often evoked by description of surrounding circumstance, and by Yeats's own philosophical reflections, as by direct portraiture. While there can be no doubt of Yeats's esteem for Synge's strength of personality as well as for his depth of vision and ability as a dramatist (an ability he recognized as exceeding his own) from the first staging of *In the Shadow of the Glen* late in 1903, and even more so after *Riders to the Sea* early in 1904, Synge's total personality as it emerges in *The Autobiography* is one that had with his death in 1909 quickly assumed legendary proportions in Yeats's mind. The passages which make up *The Death of Synge* were originally part of the diary written during the weeks immediately preceding and following Synge's death. In them Yeats attempts to evaluate with cool detachment his friend's personality, but the exalted place that Synge was finally to occupy in his mind becomes clear with the symbolic function these passages take on in the completed *Autobiography*.

The Death of Synge counterposes Synge and Lady Gregory against the Irish middle-class public. Yeats points up the motives and ideals that united his two friends, but also the differences in their personalities that ultimately contributed to Lady Gregory's victory and to Synge's destruction. He finds the intellects of both original and independent, and that this originality and independence of thought brought an almost expected abuse from the public.[34] Lady Gregory was accused of taking advantage of her position in the theater to have her own plays produced; Synge was attacked for being anti-Irish and obscene. Although both were abused, Lady Gregory's deliberateness, her respect for traditional moral values and her associations in the world of practical affairs strengthened her against this abuse. Synge, lacking Lady Gregory's associations and even her respect for at least some forms of convention, set out alone, as Lionel Johnson had done, into a wilderness of independent moral and intellectual values. "The truth is," Yeats wrote to John Quinn in 1907, the year of the *Playboy*'s premiere, "that the objection to Synge is not mainly that he makes the country people unpleasant or immoral, but that he has got a standard of morals and intellect . . . they shrink from Synge's harsh, independent, heroical, clean, wind-swept view of things."[35] Unlike Johnson, Synge was able to maintain enough intellectual aloofness to keep his will from being totally absorbed by his own subjective impulse, though this aloofness involved a reliance upon the external world characteristic of the basically objective personality. Men like Synge, Yeats said a year after the playwright's death, "have the advantage that all they write is a part of knowledge, but they are powerless before events and have often but one visible strength, the strength to reject from life and thought all that would mar their work, or deafen them in the doing of it."[36] This one strength made possible the outspoken expression of his genius. When Synge sat down to write, Yeats says in *The Autobiography*, moral conventions, practical considerations, and other writers did not exist for him. Finding in himself an unbounded intellectual and moral strength, he persisted according to his own lights, oblivious to public criticism and the subsequent emotional and physical suffering this criticism caused.[37] His obliviousness to the rest of the world and even to his own well-being was by conventional standards a deficiency seeming to rise out of an insufferable egoism, but it was for Yeats a deficiency inevitable in the artist who sacrifices everything to his genius.

Because Synge and Lady Gregory had primary natures, they looked outside themselves to the external world for their modes of artistic expression—Lady Gregory to the Kiltartan peasants and Synge to the Aran Islanders, Kerry fishermen, and vagrants of Wicklow. In the lives and dialects of these rustic Irishmen, and in the stories they told, Synge and Lady Gregory found the subjects for their art and the power of their styles. Yeats, never quite bridging the temperamental gap that divided himself from the peasants, and envying Lady Gregory and Synge their intimacy with them, had at first believed all the strange situation and character in Synge's plays to be "some overflowing of himself, or . . . mere necessity of dramatic construction," but when he read *The Aran Islands* he was delighted to discover that this situation and character was grounded in actual experience.[38] Whereas Lady Gregory developed a natural feeling of pity for the hard lives of the peasants as she became intimate with them, Synge, living with them in their cottages for extended periods of time, giving no more than he took from them and sharing as much as he could in their work, pleasures, and daily concerns, achieved a frank and equal relationship that was considerably more intimate and that would not allow for the patronizing air that such feelings of pity necessarily implied.

Synge's relationship to his Dublin audiences was another matter, but it bore, perhaps, deep-rooted elements in common with his relationship to the peasants. Yeats suggests that his emotional upset over the people's unfavorable and sometimes violent responses to his plays was due to the same kind of instinctive identification with them that he felt for his hosts in the cottages. It was certainly not due to any feeling of compassion or frustrated desire to make them happy. Yet

Yeats knew that while Synge appreciated men of genius and culture and admired the Irish peasant without bounds despite the shortcomings he was realistic enough to recognize, his diatribes against the commercial middle classes were on occasion more vituperative than Yeats's own. In his deepest affections and hostilities he could not remain aloof for all his intellectual resistance.

Yeats is certain that Synge's indignation over his public reception, whatever its psychological foundation, did not imply a diminishing of his self, but an accentuation of it. His egoism, apparent to but entirely misunderstood by the public, was minimized for his friends by a quiet and sympathetic mien and by the utter simplicity of living he greatly preferred. It was an egoism peculiar in its selflessness. His life was rich with a variety of experiences and human associations whose outward appearances were abject and colorless, but whose innate beauty his powerful sensibilities allowed him readily to discover. Expressing through these experiences and associations his own desires and affections, and raising all to symbolic power by inwardly transcending their personal immediacy, he rendered them into works of art. As Yeats puts it, he sees "himself as but a part of the spectacle of the world," mixes "into all he sees that flavour of extravagance, or of humour, or of philosophy, that makes one understand that he contemplates even his own death as if it were another's and finds in his own destiny but, as it were, a projection through a burning-glass of that general to men."[39] All became "grist for Synge's mill," but in the actual affairs of life he was but to look on and clap his hands.[40]

Synge's love and understanding of Ireland differed from Lady Gregory's in being more emotional and instinctive. Lady Gregory's life was "too energetic and complex" for her actions "to be other than deliberate,"[41] though her motivating emotions were selfless; George Moore's actions were deliberate to the point of abstraction and had his vanity to motivate them. Synge's love for his country, Yeats maintains, transcended politics; resembling Allingham's rather than Davis's, it resided in that instinctive feeling of identity rather than in ordinary patriotism, and caused him, while he remained morally and intellectually strong, and artistically independent, to react so emotionally to public abuse. Lady Gregory, whose own affinity with the people was more intellectual, sustained enough emotional distance from the crowd to view it with contempt; Moore would have reveled in the notoriety. Yeats, and Lady Gregory too, believed that the public's abuse helped to break down Synge's health, and ultimately to kill him.[42] His death hastened the collapse of those lyric ideals with which the Irish National Theatre was begun, ideals sacrificed after not too many years to the dramatic realism the public demanded. But in fact it was Synge's own realism that began to move the theater in the direction it was ultimately to take, and the public, it seems, although not appreciating his lyricism, was not ready to accept the depth or frankness of his realism either, as it was not ready to accept O'Casey's later. Indeed, it was for their realism that both Synge and O'Casey were attacked. Ironically enough, each playwright in his own time, while causing riots and being abused by the pubic, may have saved the life of the theater by filling it with patrons when they were most needed.

Lady Gregory's mild compromise with convention and Synge's absolute unwillingness to allow its considerations to dilute his vision are manifest in their work. Lady Gregory's compassion reveals itself in her plays where the peasant is made noble or endearing by his simplicity, "where the wickedest people seem but bold children." The peasant may be noble or endearing in Synge's plays too, but these qualities are often obscured behind the semi-grotesque natures of real peasants as he knew them. Synge expressed an Ireland that patriotic

Irishmen did not always expect or wish to see, certainly one that they could neither understand nor appreciate as he did; he discovered the beauty and nobility of Ireland through the weeds as well as the flowers that make up Irish life.[43]

Both Lady Gregory, imaging unity of culture in her work and in her mode of living, and Synge, displaying uncompromisingly a harsh but beautiful reality as seen through the poet's eyes, are given symbolic character in Yeats's expression of his dream. If unity of culture were to come to Ireland, both would have symbolically prefigured its advent. Their symbolic roles add weight to Yeats's later statement to the Swedish Royal Academy: "When your King gave me medal and diploma, two forms should have stood, one at either side of me, an old woman sinking into the infirmity of age and a young man's ghost."[44] Here he has brought together in their natural affinity the "great lady" and the poet. Perhaps, even, by imagining himself standing between them, he envisages the qualities of both his friends symbolically coming together in himself.

Yeats tells us that *The Bounty of Sweden* is a record of his first impressions of Stockholm, written "as in a kind of diary."[45] By saying as much he suggests, as in the other books following *Dramatis Personae,* that these disconnected passages are to be read without expectation of an overall coherence. Moreover, the statement again serves to disarm his critics, here in regard to what would certainly, and rightly, be considered an overly idealistic view of Swedish culture. Without entirely rejecting Yeats's assertion that his book is an impressionistic record (he had, after all, written it almost immediately upon his return from Sweden, but then he had also written to Lady Gregory that he intended it as part of his autobiography) we may say that its narrative continuity gives *The Bounty of Sweden* a more clearly defined structure than that of either *Estrangement* or *The Death of Synge.* And his idealistic viewpoint serves his overall design: the book proclaims in nearly every detail Yeats's delight in having discovered a nation on the verge of achieving that unity of culture for which he had been seeking so many years in Ireland. He was in fact prepared to find this achievement in Scandinavia long before any visit to Sweden had ever been projected. As early as 1900 he had written in *Beltaine,* the organ of the Irish Literary Theatre: "It is only at the awakening—as in ancient Greece, or in Elizabethan England, or in contemporary Scandinavia—that great numbers of men understand that a right understanding of life and of destiny is more important than amusement."[46] This he wrote despite his disapproval of Ibsen's realism. Now, in his actual visit to Sweden, he was able to bring living authority both to his early assertion and to his abiding Irish dream. Every experience recounted in *The Bounty of Sweden* elicits another manifestation of the cultivated nation which might be directly contrasted with the Irish, and English, experience recounted in earlier parts of *The Autobiography.*

Where for example, in *Reveries* he had complained of an Irish educational system that produced only thirsty minds "parched by many examinations," and in *The Death of Synge* that "The education of our Irish secondary schools . . . substitutes pedantry for taste," his first conversation after leaving England centers on Danish education that makes "examinations almost nothing and the personality of the teacher almost everything" and that rouses "the imagination with Danish literature and history."[47] He undoubtedly also recalled his school days in England, where class snobbishness was the rule and where the virtues of a superficial gentility were taught in place of morality, in contrast with an educational system so democratically conceived, he says, that housemaid, professor, and royalty might be good friends within the same intellectual community, and where the quality of the education was so fine that each might continue to live without awkwardness as housemaid, professor, or royalty.

Contrasting also with Yeats's earlier experience as he presents it in *The Autobiography*, was Swedish society's recognition of the artist's values. In Ireland and in England the artist had been at best tolerated as an eccentric, at worst driven to self-destruction; Yeats, whether pursuing a higher reality with his friends during the nineties, trying to impose artistic excellence as the guideline for the Irish cultural movement, or working as director of the Abbey Theatre, had always the philistine mob for his most formidable enemy. The people's attitude toward art, as toward politics, he says, sprung from a hatred that produced in them a kind of sterility: "They contemplate all creative power as the eunuchs contemplate Don Juan as he passes through Hell on the white horse."[48] In Sweden, on the other hand, Prince Eugene chose to identify himself at the dedication of the Stockholm Town Hall as one of the artist-workers (which he was) rather than as royalty.

In Ireland and England deference to public opinion turned all popular art to mediocrity or actual ugliness. Authority was lacking. "Our modern public arts," Yeats says, "architecture, plays, large decorations, have too many different tastes to please. Some taste is sure to dislike and to speak its dislike everywhere, and then because of the silence of the rest . . . there is general timidity."[49] But Stockholm had an architecture "as impressive as that of Paris, or of London," though controlled by "a vast, dominating, unconfused outline, a masterful simplicity," and all seemed "premeditated and arranged."[50] Further contributing to the enlightened Swedish attitude was the arrival of Swedish Impressionism, which was concurrent, he says, with "an intellectual awaking of the whole people," and which taught them "to see and feel . . . all those things that are as wholesome as rain and sunlight"; Swedish painters appealed to a commonly held emotion, their work being sought enthusiastically by all of "educated Stockholm." The adjective is important and bears the implication of Scandinavian quality in education, Sweden's being as impressive as Denmark's. Yeats had spent vast energies struggling for an art other than that which appealed to a badly educated Irish public.

He was fascinated, too, by Swedish Impressionism's strong "feeling for particular places."[51] He had himself insisted earlier in *The Autobiography* upon the importance of specific Irish settings for poems and plays, had praised his brother's painting "Memory Harbour" for the vivid recollection of Rosses Point it had evoked, and criticized Shelley and Morris for not using native settings in their poetry. These settings, or landscapes, included more than simple topographical features; they involved also an entire syndrome encompassing the natives' legends, values, customs, and forms of expression.[52] Thus, the Swedish Impressionists' "feeling for particular places" enriched their painting by enabling them to express a comprehensive and diverse, and at the same time "rooted" culture. By expressing this culture they could transcend it.

Along with its heightened values in education and in art, Swedish society itself had a flexibility, according to Yeats, that allowed it to recognize a man on the basis of his individual merit, the democratic attitudes toward education making possible real congeniality among all ranks. Moreover, he finds no evidence here of dominating abstract principles like those dividing Irishmen who, aside from certain opinions, might have found each other congenial companions. At the same time the decidedly undemocratic institution, Sweden's aristocracy based on "hereditary honour," provided an atmosphere of youth, beauty, and elegance found in large measure only among men of leisure and of old family traditions. So impressive a combination of beauty, individual accomplishment, and traditional distinction is possible, Yeats says, neither in a closed society like England's, nor in a democratic one like America's where individual achievement alone is the means of entry, nor in intellectual Ireland where, for example in George Russell's circle, "everybody [was] either too tall or too short, crooked or lop-sided."[53] It is conceivable only at an enlightened court like the one he found in Sweden or in the pages of Castiglione's *Courtier*.[54]

Ritual and ceremony were a fundamental part of Yeats's vision, and are almost all he chooses to recall of the Nobel Prize presentation and the palace reception afterwards. He had been attracted many years earlier to the Order of the Golden Dawn largely because of its emphasis on ritual, and had spent years seeking a ritual for his own philosophical Order. The traditions of old houses and families, too, like those he had come to know at Lissadell for instance, and more particularly at Coole, were built upon ritual and ceremony. This is not a matter of certain kinds of ceremonies, however, as the occult rituals were, but rather, as his daughter has recently expressed it, "A sense of ceremony . . . ceremony as an approach to things."[55] He had expressed a wish that she might some day herself be immersed in it:

> And may her bridegroom bring her to a house
> Where all's accustomed, ceremonious;
> For arrogance and hatred are the wares
> Peddled in the thoroughfares.
> How but in custom and in ceremony
> Are innocence and beauty born?
> Ceremony's a name for the rich horn,
> And custom for the spreading laurel tree.[56]

It is the "ceremony of innocence" whose continued existence he feared for in "The Second Coming." Custom and ceremony at the Swedish Court were exemplary.

All the accomplishments of Swedish culture converge on

the Stockholm Town Hall, which Yeats makes the symbol of
Swedish success. He had long before foreseen the need for
something like it in Ireland, if not as a symbol of accomplishment, at least as a model for inspiration. The idea, entered
originally in his diary, is repeated in *Estrangement*:

> You cannot keep the idea of a nation alive where there are no na-
> tional institutions to reverence, no national success to admire, with-
> out a model of it in the mind of the people. You can call it
> "Cathleen ni Houlihan" or the "Shan van Voght" in a mood of
> simple feeling, and love that image, but for the general purposes of
> life you must have a complex mass of images, something like an
> architect's model.[57]

The Stockholm Town Hall provided the Swedes with their
"complex mass of images." It was in Yeats's mind the result
of one overriding ideal which demanded the use, and especially the freedom of the best artists available. The building, he says, making its symbolic value emphatic, "carries
the mind backward to Byzantium." His allusion is to early
Byzantium, under the reign of Justinian in the sixth century,
when formal Roman architecture gave way to "an architecture that suggests the Sacred City in the Apocalypse of St.
John."[58] Even his image depicting the Town Hall's "mosaic-
covered walls of the 'Golden Room'" suggests Byzantium's
"gold mosaic of a wall" in "Sailing to Byzantium."[59] For Yeats
the structure's Byzantine splendor is rivaled only by the architecture of the Italian Renaissance, where civilization had
approximated unity of culture more closely than at any other
time, where "intellect and emotion, *primary* curiosity and the
antithetical dream, are for the moment one."[60] In *A Vision* the
Christian Era represents an entire historical cycle of which each
of its halves is an entire historical cycle also; wheels turn within
wheels. Byzantium had attained a zenith of cultural achievement in the first millennium comparable to that of the Italian
Renaissance in the second. By linking the Stockholm Town
Hall to Byzantium and the Italian Renaissance, Yeats confers

upon it, and upon the civilization responsible for its creation, the ultimate praise, for in these two historical moments the imagination and intellect of Western man had brought him to the fullest statement of himself.

The Irish literary movement, Yeats believed, had tried to give Ireland a model on which it could build the unity of culture that the Stockholm Town Hall symbolized. Unity of culture, the thing itself, had been accomplished only on a small scale at Coole, but in a whole nation in Sweden. Yeats was never able to accomplish as much for Ireland and eventually gave up the attempt,[61] but he was convinced that Ireland might some day find it "in the work of Lady Gregory, of Synge, of O'Grady, of Lionel Johnson, in my own work." In all, he says, "a school of journalists with simple moral ideas could find right building material to create a historical and literary nationalism as powerful as the old and nobler."[62] In his lecture before the Swedish Royal Academy, Yeats sees his own work as in some degree representing "The Irish Dramatic Movement," itself, perhaps, the most successfully realized part of the total literary movement. With his recollections before the Royal Academy he turns his confrontation of unity of culture in Sweden back on his dream for Ireland.[63] Sweden too, like the image created at Coole by Lady Gregory, and like that in Synge's plays, has in the apparently worldly method of the later books been raised to a symbolic entity.

The Autobiography begins as if it were the beginning of the world. It closes, in Yeats's vision of unity of culture as the ultimate stage in the world's spiritual evolution, as if the apocalypse had at least drawn nearer. His own history, the history of the world, and even "Translunar Paradise" are bodied forth by his imagination, and made to impinge on each other. Unity of culture would come to Ireland as it had come to Byzantium, to Italy in the fifteenth century, and to Sweden, in a great variety of human interests and beliefs disciplined and fused by a symbolic art.

NOTES   INDEX

NOTES

References to works by W. B. Yeats are, unless otherwise noted, to the following editions:

The Autobiography (New York: Macmillan, 1953). In the notes, only the titles of individual sections of this work—"Reveries Over Childhood and Youth," "The Trembling of the Veil," "Dramatis Personae," "Estrangement," "The Death of Synge," and "The Bounty of Sweden"—are cited, but all page references are to this edition unless otherwise noted.

Essays and Introductions (New York: Macmillan, 1961).

Explorations, selected by Mrs. W. B. Yeats (London: Macmillan, 1962).

Mythologies (New York: Macmillan, 1959).

The three collections above are used rather than earlier editions of the essays because they are more readily available to the reader.

The Letters of W. B. Yeats, ed. Allan Wade (London: Rupert Hart-Davis, 1954).

The Variorum Edition of the Poems of W. B. Yeats, ed. Peter Allt and Russell K. Alspach (New York: Macmillan, 1957).

A Vision (New York: Macmillan, 1961).

Copies of all unpublished material used in this book, with the exception of "Memoirs," have been made available to me by Professor Richard Ellmann. "Memoirs" has been made available to me on microfilm by the Houghton Library, Harvard University. The original manuscripts are in the possession of Mrs. W. B. Yeats, Dublin, with the exception of a manuscript book beginning April 7, 1921, which is in the National Library, Dublin.

One: THE NEED FOR SELF-PORTRAITURE

1. Quoted by John Eglinton, *A Memoir of AE* (London: Macmillan, 1937), p. 110.

2. Lecture entitled "Friends of my Youth," delivered on March 9, 1910, in London (probably at the home of Sir Arthur Birch, with Edmund Gosse presiding) from notes dictated in Dublin. The notes are unpublished.

3. Richard Ellmann, *Yeats: The Man and the Masks* (New York: Macmillan, 1948), p. 2.

4. "The Trembling of the Veil," p. 68.

5. Letter to Lady Elizabeth Pelham, *Letters,* p. 922.

6. *Ibid.,* p. 684.

7. *Ibid.,* p. 691.

8. *Ibid.,* p. 820.

9. The visual quality of the work impressed George Russell, though he had other things to complain of: "When W. B. Yeats's first section of autobiography, *Reveries Over Childhood and Youth,* appeared in 1915 [*sic*], his oldest friend George Russell . . . complained that this was no autobiography at all, but a chronological arrangement of pictures" (Ellmann, *The Man and the Masks,* p. 21).

10. See Ellmann, *The Man and the Masks,* pp. 2-3, for mythical events composed out of Yeats's own life. For myths of larger scope, see Yeats's own *Mythologies* and *A Vision,* whose cyclical periods he referred to as "stylistic arrangements of experience" (*A Vision,* p. 25). Quotations from *A Vision,* by W. B. Yeats, are reprinted with permission of Mr. M. B. Yeats and Macmillan & Co. Ltd., and of The Macmillan Company. © The Macmillan Company 1961.

11. *Letters,* p. 526.

12. Bradford, *Yeats at Work* (Carbondale and Edwardsville, Ill.: Southern Illinois University Press, 1965), p. 338. The passage in the letter to Florence Farr runs as follows: "I have a large MS book in which I write stray notes on all kinds of things. These will make up into essays. They will amuse you very much. They are quite frank and the part that cannot be printed while I am alive is the amusing part" (*Letters,* p. 526).

13. Bradford, *Yeats at Work,* p. 340.

14. Curtis Bradford, "The Speckled Bird: A Novel by W. B. Yeats," *Irish Writing,* 31 (Summer 1955), 9.

15. "Trembling of the Veil," p. 226.

16. "Reveries Over Childhood and Youth," pp. 39, 63 (see chap. iii, n. 17, below).

17. Letter of August 7, 1909, *Letters,* p. 534.

18. *A Vision* (London: T. Werner Laurie, 1925), p. 129.

19. Diary entry, March 1909; "Certain Noble Plays of Japan," *Essays and Introductions,* p. 235. And in verse, from "A Prayer for Old Age" (*Variorum Poems,* p. 553):

> God guard me from those thoughts men think
> In the mind alone;
> He that sings a lasting song
> Thinks in a marrow-bone.

Cf. Richard Ellmann's section on "affirmative capability" in *The Identity of Yeats* (New York: Oxford University Press, 1954), pp. 238-245. Quotations from *The Variorum Edition of the Poems of W. B. Yeats,* edited by Peter Allt and Russell K. Alspach, are reprinted with permission of Mr. M. B. Yeats and Macmillan & Co. Ltd., and of The Macmillan Company. Copyright 1903, 1906, 1907, 1912, 1916, 1918, 1919, 1924, 1928, 1931, 1933, 1934, 1935, 1940, 1944, 1945, 1946, 1950, 1956, 1957 by The Macmillan Company.

20. "Yeats: The Poet as Myth-Maker," *The Permanence of Yeats,* ed. James Hall and Martin Steinman (New York: Macmillan, 1950), p. 70.

21. Diary entry made August 7, 1909.

22. "Discoveries," *Essays and Introductions,* p. 292.

23. "Discoveries: Second Series," ed. Curtis Bradford, *Massachusetts Review,* 5 (Winter 1964), 301.

24. Letter to J. B. Yeats, August 5, 1913, *Letters,* p. 583.

25. *Ibid.,* p. 586.

26. Letter of November 11, 1913, quoted by Joseph Hone in *W. B. Yeats* (London: Macmillan, 1962), p. 273.

27. "Reveries," p. 51.

28. *Letters,* p. 564.

29. See pp. 108-109, this book.

30. See p. 117, this book.

31. *Variorum Poems,* p. 321.

32. Quoted by Hone, *W. B. Yeats,* p. 288.

33. Yeats's preface to J. B. Yeats's *Early Memories: Some Chapters of Autobiography* (Dundrum: Cuala Press, September 1923). Six

of his father's essays were later collected and published with an appreciation by AE in *Essays Irish and American* (Dublin: Talbot Press, and London: T. Fisher Unwin, 1918).

34. *Letters*, p. 571. J. B. Yeats's autobiography was, in fact, begun but never completed. The fragments were put in order by Yeats shortly after his father's death and published by the Cuala Press in 1923 as *Early Memories: Some Chapters of Autobiography*.

35. "Reveries," p. 2.

36. "Some New Letters from W. B. Yeats to Lady Gregory," ed. Donald Torchiana and Glenn O'Malley, *Review of English Literature*, 4 (July 1963), 44.

37. *Letters*, p. 684. J. B. Yeats had died in New York the preceding February.

Two: PUBLISHING HISTORY

1. Bradford in *Yeats at Work*, pp. 346-347, lists changes between a "corrected partial typescript found in Dublin" and the Cuala Press edition, the most interesting of which are the removal of "passages that might give offense to his family," and one concerning his own sexual awakening.

2. *Letters*, p. 599.

3. See J. M. Synge, *Prose*, Vol. II of *Collected Works*, ed. Alan Price (London: Oxford University Press, 1966), 3-15.

4. *Letters*, pp. 589, 603.

5. Bradford, *Yeats at Work*, p. 348.

6. Quoted in Ellmann, *The Man and the Masks*, p. 216.

7. Letters of December 6, 1926, and July 23, 1933, in *Letters*, pp. 721, 812.

8. *Ibid.*, p. 820.

9. Bradford in *Yeats at Work*, pp. 354-355, lists changes between two manuscripts and the Cuala Press edition. These include the suppression of passages on Maud Gonne, on Edwin Ellis's bizarre domestic life, and one which pictures Madame Blavatsky mocking her disciples. Most of this material appears in "Memoirs," but was too personal to be published. There were also some added passages. Still another suppressed passage (quoted by Bradford, p. 355) concerning T. W. Rolleston is particularly interesting when compared

with the passage suppressed from the *Savoy* essay "Verlaine in 1894" (April 1896) as it appears in "The Tragic Generation." See chap. v, n. 15, below.

10. Letter of August 1, 1921; *Letters,* p. 672.

11. Letter of December 22, 1921, *ibid.,* p. 675.

12. Letter of June 10, 1921, *ibid.,* p. 669.

13. Letter of July 1, 1921, *ibid.,* p. 671.

14. Bradford traces changes from various manuscripts for the entire book, treating "Ireland After Parnell" (because of the abundance of available material) in particular detail (*Yeats at Work,* pp. 356-372). With a few exceptions, which I shall take up elsewhere, these are relatively minor changes in style, organization, or emphasis.

15. *Explorations,* p. 107.

16. Letter of January 13, 1924, *Letters,* p. 701.

17. *Yeats at Work,* pp. 339-346.

18. "A General Introduction for my Work," *Essays and Introductions,* p. 509.

19. Yeats says that "Memoirs come down to 1896 or thereabouts"; they are actually carried into 1898.

20. *Yeats at Work,* pp. 347-348.

21. "The Trembling of the Veil," pp. 223, 224.

22. *The Autobiography,* p. 342.

23. *Letters,* p. 721.

24. *Ibid.,* p. 733.

25. *Ibid.,* pp. 818, 820.

Three: EXFOLIATION

1. "Reveries," p. 3.

2. *Ibid.,* pp. 11, 46.

3. *Ibid.,* p. 18.

4. *Ibid.,* p. 25.

5. *Ibid.,* pp. 19, 18.

6. Synge, *Prose,* p. 3.

7. *Variorum Poems,* p. 269.

8. *Ibid.,* p. 270.

9. "The Trembling of the Veil," p. 86.

10. Unpublished essay by J. B. Yeats, dated March 1916.

11. Letter of December 31, 1869, in J. B. Yeats, *Letters to his Son W. B. Yeats and Others,* ed. Joseph Hone (New York: Dutton, 1946), p. 48.

12. *A Vision,* p. 88.

13. *Letters,* p. 589.

14. "Reveries," p. 50.

15. In "Reveries," pp. 44-45, he writes: "Once when staying with my uncle at Rosses Point . . . I called upon a cousin towards midnight and asked him to get his yacht out, for I wanted to find what sea birds began to stir before dawn . . . I had wanted the birds' cries for the poem that became fifteen years afterwards 'The Shadowy Waters,' and it had been full of observation had I been able to write it when I first planned it. I had found again the windy light that moved me when a child."

16. *Ibid.,* p. 39.

17. "He never read me a passage because of its speculative interest, and indeed did not care at all for poetry where there was generalisation or abstraction however impassioned . . . He did not care even for a fine lyric passage unless he felt some actual man behind its elaboration of beauty, and he was always looking for the lineaments of some desirable, familiar life . . . All must be an idealisation of speech, and at some moment of passionate action or somnambulistic reverie" (*ibid.,* pp. 39-40).

In a letter to George Russell of May, 1900, Yeats writes: "I do not understand what you mean when you distinguish between the word that gives your idea and the more beautiful word. Unless you merely mean that beauty of detail must be subordinate to general effect, it seems to me just as if one should say 'I don't mind whether my sonata is musical or not so long as it conveys my idea.' Beauty is the end and law of poetry. It exists to find the beauty in all things, philosophy, nature, passion,—in what you will, and in so far as it rejects beauty it destroys its own right to exist. If you want to give ideas for their own sake write prose. In verse they are subordinate to beauty which is their soul. Isn't this obvious?" (*Letters,* p. 343).

18. "Reveries," p. 54.

19. Again affirming his father's censure, Yeats had written in the copy of *Ideas of Good and Evil* that he gave to John Quinn: "I think the best of these Essays is that on Shakespeare. It is a family

exasperation with the Dowden point of view, which rather filled Dublin in my youth. There is a good deal of my father in it, though nothing is just as he would have put it" (Allan Wade, *A Bibliography of the Writings of W. B. Yeats* [London: Rupert Hart-Davis, 1958], p. 88).

As Ian Fletcher points out, J. B. Yeats disapproved of Yeats's use of Dowden in *Reveries*, saying that he presented "Dowden deliberately and exclusively from a personal and didactic point of view," that he submitted "Dowden to a contrived biographical pattern" ("Rhythm and Pattern in *Autobiographies*," in *An Honoured Guest*, ed. Denis Donoghue and J. R. Mulryne [London: Edward Arnold, 1965], pp. 171-172). While he had been generally careful not to write anything that might offend either his father's sensibilities or Dowden's family, with whom he was still friendly, Yeats was somewhat concerned over certain passages in *Reveries* (see *Letters*, pp. 602, 605). But in *The Trembling of the Veil*, with his father dead, he goes on to speak of his break with Dowden with more assurance.

20. "Reveries," p. 26.

21. *Ibid.*, p. 48.

22. *Ibid.*, p. 40. Ellmann in *The Man and the Masks*, p. 29, describes some of this early unpublished verse: "The unpublished verse of the first two or three years of creative activity reveals heterogeneous efforts in several styles. The favorite scene is, as one would expect, soliloquy. There are several attempts at playwriting, usually with Spenserian characters (knights, shepherds and shepherdesses, enchanters and enchantresses) and scenery (gardens, islands) and often with Shelleyan attitudes. The hero is 'proud and solitary,' contemptuous of the crowd, Promethean, sad."

23. *Ibid.*, p. 35.

24. Yet to put the theory into practice was difficult. He says in the 1915 edition of *Reveries Over Childhood and Youth* (Dundrum: Cuala Press, 1915), p. 126, that the rejection of all words and constructions furnished by poetic convention "made it hard to write at all." "Then, too," he continues, "how hard it was to be sincere, not to make the emotion more beautiful and more violent or the circumstance more romantic."

25. "Reveries," p. 53.

26. Writing to his father on February 23, 1910, he said that he has come to "realize with some surprise how fully my philosophy of

life has been inherited from you in all but its details and applications" (*Letters*, p. 549).

27. The Hermetic Society met for the first time on June 16, 1885, with Yeats as chairman. In his opening speech he becomes strongly emotional in his reaction against the notion that "European science" is answering "all these problems." Science has not solved the problem of the soul of man, he says, but where spiritualism "is wise it will tell you that year by year the footfall grows softer on the haunted stairway, that year by year the mysterious breath becomes fainter and fainter, that every decade takes something from the vividness of the haunting shadow till it has grown so faint that none but the keenest eyes can see the feeble outline and then it is gone it is dead dead forever" (quoted by Ellmann, in *The Man and the Masks,* p. 42).

28. *The Celtic Twilight* is filled with these stories and many of Yeats's early poems were inspired by them. There are several poems about the fairies not included in the definitive edition, and "The Stolen Child," which speaks of fairies kidnapping a "human child," is filled with the names of places around Sligo: Sleuth (or Slish) Wood on the shore of Lough Gill, Rosses, the waterfall at Glen Car (*Variorum Poems,* p. 86). The island of Innisfree was the setting for a romantic legend involving a girl, her lover, and a monster. Yeats does not remember whether he "chose the island because of its beauty or for the story's sake" ("Reveries," p. 44).

29. "If I Were Four-and-Twenty," *Explorations,* p. 263.

30. "Reveries," p. 55.

31. *Ibid.,* p. 56.

32. "The Indian Upon God" and "The Indian to his Love," both of 1886, and "Anashuya and Vijaya," possibly of 1887 (Ellmann, *The Identity of Yeats,* p. 287). Also "Quatrains and Aphorisms," 1885-86, and "Kanva On Himself," written before 1889. The poem "Mohini Chatterjee" came much later.

33. *Variorum Poems,* pp. 76-77.

34. *Ibid.,* pp. 77-78.

35. The "Catholic friend" who brought him was Katharine Tynan who, she says, participated in the seance unwillingly. She tells the story in *Twenty-Five Years: Reminiscences* (London: Smith, Elder & Co., 1913), p. 208, the only difference between her account and Yeats's being that she says the spirits pointed her out as a disturbing influence and she was therefore asked to leave (which

she did, "cheerfully"), whereas Yeats remembers her during the most violent part "saying a Paternoster and Ave Maria in the corner." The violence of the effect on Yeats frightened him too, however ("Reveries," p. 64).

36. "The Trembling of the Veil," p. 129.

37. See Ellmann, *The Man and the Masks*, p. 46.

38. "Reveries," p. 62.

39. *Reveries* (Dundrum, 1915), pp. 123-125.

40. From "The Speckled Bird," quoted by Curtis Bradford, "The Speckled Bird: A Novel by W. B. Yeats," *Irish Writing*, 31 (Summer 1955), 10. This short essay introduces a fragment from the unfinished novel, pp. 12-18. Also quoted by Joseph Hone in an editorial note attached to another fragment of the novel in *The Bell*, 1 (March 1941), 24.

A like figure comes to Katharine Tynan's mind when she imagines what his childhood must have been like among the Sligo relatives: "He must have suffered all through his youth from being unlike his fellows: a white blackbird among the others, a genius among the commonplace. Probably the Anglo-Irish milieu in which he grew up was the least sympathetic he could have found. The Anglo-Irishman, although he achieves great things at times, is, in the rank and file of him, somewhat harsh. He has the John Bullish attitude towards sentimentality without the real sentiment which John Bull is unaware of possessing, although it jumps to the eye of everyone else. He has somewhat of the Celt's irritability and jealousy: in fact, these things grafted upon him make for an intolerance which is far from being Celtic" (*Twenty-Five Years*, p. 144).

41. His Sligo childhood may, in fact, have been somewhat harsher than *Reveries* suggests (see n. 40, above). J. B. Yeats also suggests as much in a letter to his wife (who was staying in Sligo with the children) from London on November 1, 1872, when he speaks of "dictatorial Aunts," and says that "Willy is sensitive, intellectual and emotional, very easily rebuffed and continually afraid of being rebuffed so that with him one has to use sensitiveness which is so rare at Merville." Separate fragments of this letter appear in J. B. Yeats's *Letters*, ed. Hone, p. 50, and Hone's *W. B. Yeats*, p. 17.

42. *Letters*, p. 140.

43. *Variorum Poems*, pp. 64-67.

44. Letter to Katharine Tynan, January 31, 1889, *Letters,* p. 106.

45. "Reveries," p. 54.

46. *Ibid.,* p. 62.

47. *Twenty-Five Years,* pp. 143-145.

48. "Reveries," p. 65. An explanation of Yeats's weighing all life in the scales of his own life can be found in *On The Boiler* (Dublin: Cuala Press, 1939), p. 22: "I discover all these men [his ancestors] in my single mind, think that I myself have gone through the same vicissitudes, that I am going through them all at this very moment, and wonder if the balance has come right; then I go beyond those minds and my single mind and discover that I have been describing everybody's struggle, and the gyres turn in my thoughts. Vico was the first modern philosopher to discover in his own mind, and in the European past, all human destiny. 'We can know nothing,' he said, 'that we have not made.' Swift, too, Vico's contemporary, in his first political essay saw history as a personal experience, so too did Hegel in his 'Philosophy of History'; Balzac in his letter to the Duchesse de Castris, and here and there in 'Le Peau de Chagrin' and 'Catherine de Medici.' "

Four: THE SEARCH FOR UNITY

1. "If I Were Four-and-Twenty," *Explorations,* p. 263.

2. "The Trembling of the Veil," p. 70.

3. See pp. 67 and 26, this book.

4. Quoted in Ellmann, *The Man and the Masks,* p. 238.

5. *Explorations,* p. 280.

6. "The Trembling of the Veil," p. 72.

7. Yeats had quoted her as saying, "When a man begins to make love to me I instantly see it as a stage performance." As told by Mrs. W. B. Yeats in "A Foreward to the Letters of W. B. Yeats" in *Florence Farr, Bernard Shaw, W. B. Yeats: Letters,* ed. Clifford Bax (London: Home & Van Thal, 1946), p. 34.

8. Cf. *A Vision,* pp. 156-157.

9. The fragmentation of Henley's personality is stated more candidly in "Memoirs" than in *The Autobiography* when Yeats says that his devotion to his disciples was at least partly to compensate for his own physical and artistic inadequacies: "Lame from

syphilis, always ailing, and with no natural mastery of written words, he perhaps tried to find his expression in us, and therefore all but loved us as himself."

10. Cf. Yeats's description of phase nineteen in *A Vision*, of which Wilde is an example: "This phase is the beginning of the artificial, the abstract, the fragmentary, and the dramatic. Unity of Being is no longer possible, for the being is compelled to live in a fragment of itself and to dramatise that fragment" (p. 148). And a few pages later: "I find in Wilde . . . something pretty, feminine, and insincere, derived from his admiration for writers of the 17th and earlier phases, and much that is violent, arbitrary and insolent, derived from his desire to escape . . . Here one finds men and women who love those who rob them or beat them, as though the soul were intoxicated by its discovery of human nature, or found even a secret delight in the shattering of the image of its desire. It is as though it cried, 'I would be possessed by' or 'I would possess that which is Human. What do I care if it is good or bad?' There is no 'disillusionment', for they have found that which they have sought, but that which they have sought and found is a fragment" (p. 150).

11. Yeats's various characterizations of him, in *The Autobiography* and elsewhere, are consistent in making conspicuous the absence of intellectual power. He says of Morris's portrait: "Its grave wide-open eyes, like the eyes of some dreaming beast, remind me of the open eyes of Titian's "Ariosto," while the broad vigorous body suggests a mind that has no need of the intellect to remain sane, though it give itself to every phantasy: the dreamer of the middle ages. It is 'the fool of fairy . . . wide and wild as a hill,' the resolute European image that yet half remembers Buddha's motionless meditation, and has no trait in common with the wavering, lean image of hungry speculation" ("The Trembling of the Veil," p. 87). Yeats found Morris's dream-like instinct forever underlying his judgment. Balzac was, in his mind, "the man the French Bourgeoisie read so much a few years ago"; wine was a source of inspiration. In "The Happiest of Poets," Yeats had described Morris's preference for a house as the "make-believe of a child who is remaking the world, not always in the same way, but always after its own heart; and so, unlike all other modern writers, he makes his poetry out of unending pictures of a happiness that is often what a child might imagine, and always a happiness that sets mind

and body at ease" (*Essays and Introductions*, pp. 60-61). His vision. then, was that of a dreamer, a child, or one divinely inspired, but never of the intellect.

12. In a review of *The Well at the World's End* he had more or less defined Morris's significance for him in terms consistent with the image in *The Autobiography:* "That Mr. William Morris was the greatest poet of his time one may doubt, remembering more impassioned numbers than his, but one need not doubt at all that he was the poet of his time who was most perfectly a poet. Certain men impress themselves on the imagination of the world as types, and Shelley, with his wayward desires, his unavailing protest, has become the type of the poet to most men and to all women, and perhaps because he seemed to illustrate that English dream, which holds the poet and the artist unfitted for practical life: laughable and lovable children whose stories and angers one may listen to when the day's work is done. If, however, a time come when the world recognises that the day's work, that practical life, become noble just in so far as they approach the dream of the poet and the artist, then Mr. William Morris may become, instead of Shelley, the type of the poet: for he more than any man of modern days tried to change the life of his time into the life of his dream . . . Almost alone among the dreamers of our time, he accepted life and called it good; and because almost alone among them he saw, amid its incompleteness and triviality, the Earthly Paradise that shall blossom at the end of the ages" ("Mr. William Morris and his Tale of Beauty," *Bookman* [New York], 4 [January 1897], 456-457).

13. "The Trembling of the Veil," p. 87.

14. Bradford reports a textual error here which was never put right. In the manuscripts of "Four Years" Yeats has Nettleship "defend his 'lion pictures' as follows: 'Everybody should have a *raison d'être*,' was one of his phrases. 'Mrs. E—'s articles are not good but they are her *raison d'être*,' and, another day, 'My lion pictures are my *raison d'être*.' Without the last clause, which has already dropped out of the Cuala Press edition, the anecdote has lost its point" (*Yeats at Work*, p. 355). Yeats it seems was not convinced by Nettleship's justification of his lion pictures.

15. He makes this explicit in "Memoirs": "Madame Blavatsky herself had as much of my admiration as William Morris and I admired them for the same reason. They had more human nature

than anybody else; they at least were unforeseen, illogical, incomprehensible. Perhaps I escaped when I was near them from the restlessness of my own mind."

16. Yeats had little regard for most of Madame Blavatsky's followers and implies in *The Autobiography* that she shared his feelings. He disapproved of their self-righteousness as he did that of the Socialists at Kelmscott House and speaks of them condescendingly in his "Esoteric Sections Journal" as well as in *The Autobiography:* "As to the personnel of sections . . . They seem some intellectual, one or two cultural, the rest the usual amorphous material that gathers round all new things—All amorphous and clever alike have much zeal—and here and there a few sparkles of fanaticism are visible" (quoted in Ellmann, *The Man and the Masks,* p. 66). In a letter to John O'Leary written in 1888, he described one "second sighted" member as a fool (*Letters,* p. 57). And to Katharine Tynan he satirically expressed concern over a "sad accident": "A sad accident happened at Madame Blavatsky's lately, I hear. A big materialist sat on the astral double of a poor young Indian. It was sitting on the sofa and he was too material to be able to see it. Certainly a sad accident!" (*Letters,* p. 59).

17. Yeats says in "The Trembling of the Veil" that he was initiated into the Order of the Golden Dawn in May or June 1887, but according to Virginia Moore the date was March 7, 1890. See *The Unicorn* (New York: Macmillan, 1954), p. 27.

18. *Essays and Introductions,* p. 154.

19. "The Trembling of the Veil," p. 116.

20. Thomas R. Whitaker in *Swan and Shadow: Yeats's Dialogue With History* (Chapel Hill, N.C.: University of North Carolina Press, 1959), p. 30, has pointed out an analogue and possible source of this historical view in John Eglinton's *Two Essays on the Remnant* (Dublin, 1894), p. 14. Whitaker quotes: "In the time of Chaucer the English nation is as fair as a rosebud, and its poets babble of spring, but a couple of centuries later, when Queen Elizabeth was pondering whether she could not in some way restrain London's further growth, its expanded petals were falling away in a shower of dramas and epics."

21. "The Trembling of the Veil," p. 118.

22. *Ibid.,* p. 119.

23. *Letters,* p. 665. The first edition of "Four Years" concluded

with a short section describing the founding of the Irish Literary Society. This material was removed to "Ireland After Parnell" in the first edition of *The Trembling of the Veil.*

24. *Letters,* p. 672.

25. "The Trembling of the Veil," p. 125.

26. *Ibid.,* p. 130.

27. Maud Gonne speaks of Taylor as "a very brilliant young man with a reddish beard." She goes on to say: ". . . he and I became great friends. He was, I think, the most brilliant orator I ever heard, and defended revolutionary prisoners with splendid ability and disinterestedness. He succeeded on several occasions in defeating British law, his chief interest being in those whom he knew to be guilty under it" (Maud Gonne MacBride, *A Servant of the Queen* [Dublin: Golden Eagle Books, 1950], p. 85).

Maud Gonne, in fact, walked out of the first performance of Synge's *In the Shadow of the Glen* "in protest against what [she] regarded as a decadent intrusion where the inspiration of idealism rather than the down pull of realism was needed" (J. H. Cousins quoted by Lennox Robinson, in *Ireland's Abbey Theatre* [London: Sidgwick and Jackson, 1951], p. 36). She also resigned her vice-presidency of the Irish National Theatre Society in consequence of the play.

28. Bradford says that an early manuscript of "Ireland After Parnell" makes plain that "Yeats felt that had his plan to combine the nationalist movement with a revival of Irish culture succeeded, Hyde might have been saved from politics and that O'Grady would have had real influence on 'Irish education and nationality' " (*Yeats at Work,* p. 359).

Ann Saddlemyer has pointed up the divisive force of the Gaelic League even within Yeats's circle: Douglas Hyde and George Moore were almost fanatic in its support (though the depth of Moore's zeal may be questionable); Edward Martyn was also enthusiastic, as well as Lady Gregory whose affections were, however, divided. Yeats remained friendly without any real interest, but Synge, who was himself fluent in Irish, lived for a time with people who spoke it in their daily lives, and was inspired by it in his art, "denounced the Gaelic League as 'founded on a doctrine that is made up of ignorance, fraud, and hypocrisy' "; see Synge's "Can We Go Back Into Our Mother's Womb?", *Prose,* pp. 399-400. John Eglinton was also opposed to it; see "The Cult of the Celt: Pan-Celtism in the Nineties," *The World of W. B. Yeats: Essays in Perspective,* ed. Robin Skelton and Ann Saddlemyer (Dublin: Dolmen Press, 1965), pp. 32-33.

29. In spite of their differences, Yeats respected Taylor. This is indicated more definitely in an essay written not long after Taylor's death: "Poetry and Tradition," in *Essays and Introductions,* pp. 246-247. The clear-cut antithesis with O'Leary in *The Autobiography* serves his design, however.

30. In 1895 Yeats evidently felt progress had been made in bringing the factions together. One essay observes that Irish poets of the day "are examples of the long continued and resolute purpose of the Irish writers to bring their literary tradition to perfection, to discover fitting symbols for their emotions, or to accentuate what is at once Celtic and excellent in their nature, that they may be at last tongues of fire uttering the evangel of the Celtic peoples" ("Irish National Literature III—Contemporary Irish Poets," *Bookman* [London], 8 [September 1895], 167-170). The month before he even complimented the Irish public for its improved taste, for being "a little more exacting, a little more conscious of excellence." The credit for this too he gives to contemporary Irish writers, including some with whom he had been at odds. "Whatever be the cause," he says, "we have for the first time in Ireland, and among the Irish in England, a school of men of letters united by a common purpose, and a small but increasing public who love literature for her own sake and not as the scullery-maid of politics" ("Irish National Literature—Contemporary Prose Writers," *ibid.,* [August 1895], 138-140). Whether his enthusiasm of 1895 reflected a passing optimism that altered with new events, or whether he believed progress had in fact been made is uncertain.

31. "The Trembling of the Veil," p. 141.

32. Bradford in *Yeats at Work,* p. 366, quotes an early manuscript in which Yeats is even more sharply critical of Ireland. It was not long, however, before Yeats did establish fruitful contact with at least some of Unionist Ireland. He was welcomed by the Gore-Booths to Lissadell in 1894, and he recounts in a letter to Katharine Tynan of March 25, 1895, the fast increasing interest of Unionists, who "are much better educated than our own people, and have a better instinct for excellence," in the work of contemporary

Irish writers (*Letters,* p. 254). It was, perhaps, this encouraging situation that stimulated Yeats to write the 1895 *Bookman* essays.

33. "The Trembling of the Veil," p. 146.

34. *A Vision,* p. 173.

35. Yeats wrote to Katharine Tynan in 1906: "I once hoped a great deal from George Russell's influence . . . but he has the religious genius, and it is the essence of the religious genius, I mean the genius of the religious teacher, to look upon all souls as equal. They are never equal in the eyes of any craft, but Russell cannot bear anything that sets one man above another. He encourages everyone to write poetry because he thinks it good for their souls, and he doesn't care a rush whether it is good or bad . . . The trouble is that Russell himself is absolutely charming and all the more charming because he suffers fools gladly . . . His very mischief is a logical expression of his genius" (*Letters,* p. 477). See also "Estrangement," p. 283.

Synge had advised his friend Stephen MacKenna not to send a manuscript to both Yeats and Russell for criticism because "what one likes the other hates." See "Synge To MacKenna: The Mature Years" (a collection of letters), ed. Ann Saddlemyer, *Massachusetts Review,* 5 (Winter 1964), 292.

36. P. 176. Yeats did not always feel this way about Russell's poetry, or at least not in his first book of poems, *Homeward: Songs by the Way.* In "Irish National Literature III—Contemporary Irish Poets," he says: "AE's 'Homeward: Songs by the Way' embody . . . a continual desire for union with the spirit, a continual warfare with the world, in a symbolism that would be wholly personal but for an occasional word out of his well-beloved 'Upanishads' . . . he, more than any, has a subtle rhythm, precision of phrase, an emotional relation to form and colour, and a perfect understanding that the business of poetry is not to enforce an opinion or expound an action, but to bring us into communion with the moods and passions which are the creative powers behind the universe; that though the poet may need to master many opinions, they are but the body and the symbols for his art, the formula of evocation for making the invisible visible."

37. "The Trembling of the Veil," p. 151.

38. "William Blake and his Illustrations to the *Divine Comedy,*" *Essays and Introductions,* p. 119.

39. "Swedenborg, Mediums, and the Desolate Places," *Explorations,* p. 33.

40. "William Blake and the Imagination," *Essays and Introductions,* p. 112.

41. *The Identity of Yeats,* pp. 218-219.

42. *Essays and Introductions,* p. 28.

43. "The Philosophy of Shelley's Poetry," *ibid.,* p. 79.

44. *Mythologies,* p. 346.

45. Cf. "Per Amica Silentia Lunae," in *Mythologies,* pp. 358-361.

46. "The Trembling of the Veil," p. 163.

47. *Ibid.,* pp. 164-165. "Per Amica," *Mythologies,* p. 329.

48. Cf. Helen Hennessy Vendler, *Yeats's Vision and the Later Plays* (Cambridge, Mass.: Harvard University Press, 1963), p. 85: "It has not been said often enough that the mask is adopted in order to free creative power, that it is a condition of penetration to the *Anima Mundi.*"

49. *Mythologies,* p. 328.

50. "The Trembling of the Veil," p. 165.

51. "Ego Dominus Tuus," *Variorum Poems,* p. 371.

52. "W. B. Yeats: Variations on the Visionary Quest," *University of Toronto Quarterly,* 30 (October 1960), 79.

Five: THE TREMBLING OF THE VEIL

1. "The Trembling of the Veil," p. 174.

2. *A Vision,* p. 299. In the nineties, before the development of Yeats's mythology, and perhaps when the tragedy shortly to come was not yet apparent, he foresaw the age's turning away from abstraction, but not its passing into objectivity. He says in his laudatory and optimistic essay, "Irish National Literature III—Contemporary Irish Poets," in the *Bookman,* that "It seems to a perhaps fanciful watcher of the skies like myself that this age of criticism is about to pass, and an age of imagination, of emotion, of moods, of revelation, about to come in its place; for certainly belief in a supersensual world is at hand again." A year later, in "Miss Fiona Macleod as a Poet," *Bookman* (London), 11 (December 1896), 92-93, he notes that according to literary feeling in France, "the great change of our time is believed to be a return to the

subjective." Yeats agreed, seeing the Rhymers in England and the Symbolists in France as examples of this return.

3. He had tried to explain the dualism as early as 1892 in an essay on the Rhymers' Club in *The Boston Pilot,* before there was any outward suggestion of tragedy: "The cultivated man has begun a somewhat hectic search for the common pleasures of common men and for the rough accidents of life. The typical young poet of our day is an aesthete with a surfeit, searching sadly for his lost Philistinism, his heart full of an unsatisfied hunger for the common place. He is an Alastor tired of his woods and longing for beer and skittles." The essay is reprinted in *Letters to the New Island,* ed. Horace Reynolds (Cambridge, Mass.: Harvard University Press, 1934), p. 146. Yeats erroneously speaks of Alastor but evidently means the unnamed hero of that poem. By the end of the decade this explanation, at least partly reaction against Victorian respectability, was obviously inadequate.

Mario Praz sees the inner turmoil of the *fin de siècle* poets as a manifestation of what he calls *The Romantic Agony* (trans. Angus Davidson, London, New York, Toronto: Oxford University Press, 1951). Graham Hough, in *The Last Romantics* (London: Duckworth, 1949), p. 212, explains with a critical detachment Yeats could not possess that their failure as poets was simply because their talents were not adequate to what should have been "an age of poetical innovation," but he says nothing to explain their personal tragedies beyond what this failure implies. On the other hand, A. G. Stock, in *W. B. Yeats: His Poetry and Thought* (Cambridge, Eng.: Cambridge University Press, 1964), p. 76, has ascribed the tragedy to an unspannable gap between the artists' lives and their art. For each artist, Stock says, there was "too deep a gulf between the creative spirit in him and the life he lived, and this left him nothing to believe in, so that poetry withered and life became meaningless." The lives and poetry of many of Yeats's friends seem to justify this explanation. Yet it, like Yeats's own early explanations, perhaps tends to be facile and insufficient. It is true that these men led lives of disorder, but as we see them in "The Tragic Generation" they can hardly be described as lives of riotous pleasure contrasting with the reserve and timidity of their poetry. If their poetry revealed a melancholy spirit of disenchantment, the very wantonness of their lives revealed the same spirit.

4. Letter to J. B. Yeats, February 16, 1910, *Letters,* p. 548.

5. "The Trembling of the Veil," p. 181. Yeats wrote that Johnson's poems, too, were "perfect speech indeed but . . . still more a perfect song." (April 7, 1921, manuscript book, National Library, Dublin.) He explains in *Per Amica Silentia Lunae* why these poets, and all poets, "sing" of their own lives, morbid though they might be: "We make out of the quarrel with others, rhetoric, but of the quarrel with ourselves, poetry. Unlike the rhetoricians, who get a confident voice from remembering the crowd they have won or may win, we sing amid our uncertainty; and, smitten even in the presence of the most high beauty by the knowledge of our solitude, our rhythm shudders. I think, too, that no fine poet, no matter how disordered his life, has ever, even in his mere life, had pleasure for his end. Johnson and Dowson, friends of my youth, were dissipated men, the one a drunkard, the other a drunkard and mad about women, and yet they had the gravity of men who had found life out and were awakening from the dream" (*Mythologies*, p. 331).

6. Johnson had "renounced the joy of the world without accepting the joy of God" ("Mr. Lionel Johnson's Poems," *Bookman* [London], 13 [February 1898], 155).

7. Yeats does not appear to have read Kierkegaard, though there are other affinities between them. See Virginia Moore, *The Unicorn*, p. 435.

8. "Friends of my Youth," a 1910 lecture on contemporary poetry.

9. "Mr. Lionel Johnson's Poems," *Bookman.*

10. Letter to Lady Gregory, February 11, 1913, *Letters*, p. 575. For Beardsley, Yeats says, as for many of his contemporaries, no part of human life should remain unexpressed. Yeats had written in his diary on May 18, 1912: "When any part of human life has been left unexpressed there is a hunger for its expression in large numbers of men and if this expression is prevented artificially this hunger becomes morbid, and if the educated do not become its voice the ignorant will. From this cause have come the Victorian Charlatanic mystics and the obscene sentences, written upon the walls of jakes." In "The Tragic Generation" he goes beyond the moral issue: the artist explores what has long been forbidden for the sheer delight of doing so.

11. *A Vision*, p. 130.

12. "Memoirs."

13. "The Trembling of the Veil," p. 205.

14. "Verlaine in 1894," *The Savoy* (April 1896), 118. Yeats refers to the daimon as his "buried self" in "The Trembling of the Veil," p. 223. See Virginia Moore, *The Unicorn*, pp. 287-289.

15. "Verlaine in 1894." Bradford quotes from a second manuscript of "Four Years" a passage on Rolleston that Yeats later deleted: "He was ten years older than I, and I thought of him as a perfect leader, but all wholesome things, Wordsworthianism and the Spectator newspaper allured him to his end. He combined an interest for morals with an incapacity for moral discovery, yet who could take his eyes from watching a body that had the beauty of some Roman copy of a Greek masterpiece of the best period. He was my first public disappointment, and because of it I have tried to choose my moralists from the unwholesome edge of the Mareotic Sea where a man whips his own shadow" (*Yeats at Work*, p. 355).

16. Hough, *The Last Romantics*, p. 188.

17. Hone, *W. B. Yeats*, p. 108, note. Yeats spells it "Douchenday."

18. "The Trembling of the Veil," p. 193. *A Vision*, p. 273. Cf. Ian Fletcher, "Explorations and Recoveries—II: Symons, Yeats and the Demonic Dance," *London Magazine*, 7 (June 1960), 46-60.

19. Note to "The Hosting of the Sidhe," *Variorum Poems*, p. 800. Cf. Frank Kermode, *The Romantic Image* (London: Routledge and Kegan Paul, 1957), pp. 22-28, 58-76.

20. "The Trembling of the Veil," p. 116. "The Gyres" and "Lapis Lazuli," *Variorum Poems*, pp. 564, 565, 567. Cf. Whitaker, *Swan and Shadow*, pp. 148, 269-281.

21. Yeats's Introduction to *The Oxford Book of Modern Verse* (Oxford: Oxford University Press, 1936), pp. xxv, xxi.

22. Although the dates of the Rhymers' Club cannot be determined with absolute certainty, Albert J. Farmer, in *Le Mouvement esthetique et "decadent" en Angleterre* (Paris: Librairie Ancienne Honoré Champion, 1931), pp. 261, 268, has said that it began in 1891 and ended in 1894; this has been generally accepted.

23. Yeats infuriated his father when, infatuated by Maud Gonne's beauty, he supported what would ordinarily have been for him an untenable position of chauvinistic belligerence. And he wrote Ellen O'Leary rather light-heartedly in 1889 that Maud Gonne would "make many converts to her political belief. If she said the world was flat or the moon an old caubeen tossed up into the sky I would be proud to be of her party" (*Letters*, p. 110).

24. She did come to appreciate Yeats's nationalist work, however, though perhaps only after his death: "Being young and hasty, I secretly felt action not books was needed; I did not then realise how the written word may lead to action and I drifted off to speak at other meetings held on wild hillsides, where resistance to evictions was being organised." "Without Yeats," she says later in her eulogy, "there would have been no literary revival in Ireland," and without the literary revival, she suggests, there would have been no Easter Week and no ultimate victory ("Yeats and Ireland," *Scattering Branches: Tributes to the Memory of W. B. Yeats,* ed. Stephen Gwynn [London: Macmillan, 1940], pp. 19 and 27).

25. "The Trembling of the Veil," p. 218.

26. *Ibid.,* p. 223.

27. A devout Catholic, Martyn was furious when he learned that Yeats was making his invocations in an empty room above the chapel and he forbade him to continue; this activity might obstruct the passage of prayer. Yeats's invocations to the lunar powers were so powerful that one night Florimond de Basterot, another guest, dreamed of "Neptune so vividly that he had got out of bed and locked his door" ("Memoirs").

28. See note, "The Vision of an Archer," *The Autobiography,* p. 342.

29. See p. 30, above; and "The Trembling of the Veil," p. 224.

30. Ellmann, *The Man and the Masks,* p. 159.

31. "The Trembling of the Veil," p. 226.

32. Cf. Gerald Levin, "The Yeats of the *Autobiographies*: A Man of Phase 17," *Texas Studies in Literature and Language,* 6 (Autumn 1964), 398-405.

Six: CULTURE AS RECONCILIATION

1. *Ave* (New York: D. Appleton, 1911), p. 41.

2. *Ibid.,* pp. 45-46. And later: "There's Yeats . . . the man in the long black cloak like a Bible reader, coming out of the bun-shop" (p. 78) and, "I came upon a tall black figure standing at the edge of the lake, wearing a cloak which fell in straight folds to his knees, looking like a great umbrella forgotten by some picnic party" (p. 251).

3. *Ibid.*, pp. 55, 255, 63.

4. *Ibid.*, pp. 292-293.

5. In a 1913 entry in reaction to Moore's *English Review* article which preceded and included parts of *Vale*. The passage appears in *Vale* (New York: D. Appleton, 1914), pp. 170-172.

6. See p. 31, above.

7. "Dramatis Personae," p. 235.

8. In "Memoirs" Yeats says that Martyn had a good intellect but one which "has been always thwarted by its lack of interest in life, religious caution having kept him always on the brink of the world, in a half unwilling virginity of the feelings imaging the virginity of his body." His semi-hysterical response to religious criticism of *The Countess Cathleen* is ample testimony to the deleterious effect of this "religious caution."

9. "At my grandmother's," Yeats says in "Memoirs," "I had learned to love an elaborate house, a garden and trees, and those grey country houses, Lissadell, Hazelwood House, and the far rarely seen tower of Markee, had always called to my mind, a life set amid natural beauty and the activity of servants and labourers, who seemed themselves natural—as birds and trees are natural. No house in a town, no solitary house even, not linked to vegetation and beset by seasonal activities, has ever seemed to me but as 'the tent of the shepherd.' "

10. See "Coole Park and Ballylee, 1931" (*Variorum Poems*, p. 491):
> Beloved books that famous hands have bound,
> Old marble heads, old pictures everywhere;
> Great rooms where travelled men and children found
> Content or joy; a last inheritor
> Where none has reigned that lacked a name and fame
> Or out of folly into folly came.

It was perhaps with Coole House, already falling into ruin, partly in his mind that Yeats wrote the description of the ruined house in his play *Purgatory* (*Collected Plays* [New York: Macmillan, 1953], pp. 431-432).

11. Letter to Lady Gregory, March 8, 1909, *Letters*, p. 525. Also see "Estrangement," p. 297.

12. "Estrangement," p. 280.

13. *Ibid.*, p. 287.

14. *Vale*, p. 182.

15. "Dramatis Personae," pp. 237-238.

16. *Ibid.,* p. 238.

17. See Ellmann, *The Man and the Masks,* pp. 264-265. For examples, see "The Tower," where Yeats proudly claims kinship with Burke and Grattan (*Variorum Poems,* p. 414), and "Blood and the Moon" (*ibid.,* p. 480):

> I declare this tower is my symbol; I declare
> This winding, gyring, spiring treadmill of a stair
> is my ancestral stair;
> That Goldsmith and the Dean, Berkeley and Burke
> have travelled there.

And in a 1925 speech to the Irish Senate protesting the law against divorce: "We against whom you have done this thing are no petty people. We are one of the great stocks of Europe. We are the people of Burke; we are the people of Grattan; we are the people of Swift, the people of Emmet, the people of Parnell. We have created the most of the modern literature of this country. We have created the best of its political intelligence" (*The Senate Speeches of W. B. Yeats,* ed. Donald R. Pearce [Bloomington, Ind.: Indiana University Press, 1960], p. 99). There are numerous other examples. Donald T. Torchiana's *W. B. Yeats and Georgian Ireland* (Evanston, Ill.: Northwestern University Press, 1966) is largely devoted to Yeats's intellectual and spiritual connections with eighteenth-century Ireland.

18. *Vale,* p. 203.

19. "Dramatis Personae," p. 239.

20. *Ibid.,* p. 239.

21. *Ibid.,* p. 243.

22. *Explorations,* p. 73.

23. *A Vision,* p. 156. The possibility of an individual's being "out of phase" adds to the variety of personal traits in Yeats's mostly deterministic system. Thus two men can manifest the same phase in entirely different ways.

24. "Dramatis Personae," p. 263. Moore himself testifies to his deliberate efforts to create an image. Having been angered by Dublin's reception of *The Countess Cathleen,* he contemplated returning to England by the first boat the morning after his arrival: "But the morning boat was already in the offing; word should have been left overnight that I was to be called at seven. An impulsive departure would be in strict keeping with myself . . . a note for Yeats, enclosing a paragraph to be sent to the papers: 'Mr. George

Moore arrived in Dublin for the performance of "The Countess Cathleen," but the hissing of the play so shocked his artistic sensibilities that he could not bide another day in Dublin, and went away by the eight o'clock boat.' The right thing to do, without a doubt, only I had not done it, and to go away by the eleven o'clock boat from the North Wall would not be quite the same thing" (*Ave*, p. 106).

25. "Dramatis Personae," p. 265.

26. Yeats says in "Memoirs" that Moore "was Edward Martyn's close friend, having succeeded a certain charming, lascivious Count Slenlock lately dead of drink. I have observed in other abnormally virtuous men a tendency to choose friends for the sins they themselves had renounced."

27. "Dramatis Personae," p. 235.

28. A few years later, however, in the vociferous language of *On The Boiler* (p. 30), he saw Catholic Ireland about to play its rightful part in molding an enlightened Ireland.

29. "Dramatis Personae," p. 277; "Coole Park, 1929," *Variorum Poems,* p. 489.

30. *Mythologies,* p. 326.

31. *A Vision,* p. 170; "Dramatis Personae," p. 277.

32. "Estrangement," p. 279.

33. "The Death of Synge," p. 305.

34. "The Irish public, which has been excited into an active state of democratic envy and jealousy, will not accept the pre-eminence of one or two writers—of Lady Gregory let us say. In its present phase it dislikes, or rather the expressive part of it dislikes all individual eminence. It lacks generosity. As soon as it has helped to raise any man or woman to a position of importance, it becomes jealous . . . This feeling is increased when it recognizes in this individual, the free mind, the mind that plays with life, and expresses great things lightly. It distrusts all that is not plainly logical work. A play with a purpose or a moral let us say—is as much a part of social organization as a newspaper, or a speech. It likes to see the railway tracks of thought. It is afraid of the wilderness" (Diary entry made February 13, 1909).

35. *Letters,* p. 495.

36. "J. M. Synge and the Ireland of his Time," *Essays and Introductions,* p. 329.

37. "He was much shaken by the *Playboy* riot; on the first night confused and excited, knowing not what to do, and ill before many days, but it made no difference in his work. He neither exaggerated out of defiance nor softened out of timidity. He wrote on as if nothing had happened, altering *The Tinker's Wedding* to a more unpopular form, but writing a beautiful serene *Deirdre*, with, for the first time since his *Riders to the Sea*, no touch of sarcasm or defiance. Misfortune shook his physical nature while it left his intellect and his moral nature untroubled. The external self, the mask, the *persona*, was a shadow; character was all" (*ibid.*, p. 329). He may in fact not have been quite this detached. According to Peter Kavanagh, Synge was extremely angered by the public's reception of *In the Shadow of the Glen* and *The Well of the Saints*. He told Willie Fay, perhaps anticipating *The Playboy*, "Very well, then; the next play I write I will make sure it will annoy them" (*The Story of the Abbey Theatre* [New York: Devin-Adair, 1950], p. 57).

38. "J. M. Synge and the Ireland of his Time," *Essays and Introductions*, p. 326. Synge affirms in his preface to *The Playboy of the Western World* that the sayings and ideas in his play are all taken directly from his experience among the Irish peasants, and that they are, if anything, milder in the play than in actuality (*The Complete Works* [New York: Random House, 1935], p. 3).

39. "J. M. Synge and the Ireland of his Time," *Essays and Introductions*, p. 322. Yeats had written to Lady Gregory even in 1907 that he really did not think Synge "selfish or egotistical, but he is so absorbed in his own vision of the world that he cares for nothing else." Quoted by David H. Greene, in *J. M. Synge* (New York: Macmillan, 1959), p. 232.

40. *A Vision*, p. 168.

41. "Estrangement," p. 287.

42. Lady Gregory, *Our Irish Theatre* (New York and London: G. P. Putnam's Sons, 1914), p. 134. Synge died of Hodgkin's disease, but it is possible that the course of the disease was accelerated by the emotional disturbance. This disturbance, his biographer David Greene shows, was as much due to the turbulence of his betrothal to the actress Molly Allgood as to the *Playboy* rows.

43. "The Controversy Over *The Playboy of the Western World*," *Explorations*, p. 225.

44. "The Bounty of Sweden," p. 336.

45. *Ibid.*, p. 323.

46. "The Theatre," *Essays and Introductions*, p. 171. See also the quotation from *Samhain: 1903*, p. 27, above.

47. "Reveries," p. 56; "The Death of Synge," p. 303; "The Bounty of Sweden," p. 326.

48. "Estrangement," p. 295.

49. "The Death of Synge," p. 316.

50. "The Bounty of Sweden," p. 330.

51. *Ibid.*, p. 335.

52. He had written to Katharine Tynan as early as 1888, that "We should make poems on the familiar landscapes we love, not the strange and rare and glittering scenes we wonder at" (*Letters*, p. 99). In an essay, "What is 'Popular Poetry'?" (1901), he wrote: "one's verses should hold, as in a mirror, the colours of one's own climate and scenery in their right proportion" (*Essays and Introductions*, p. 5). Cf. Ellmann, *The Identity of Yeats*, pp. 14-16.

53. "The Death of Synge," p. 316.

54. At the Court of Urbino where "youth for certain brief years imposed upon drowsy learning the discipline of its joy" ("The Bounty of Sweden," p. 332).

Nine years after the publication of *The Bounty of Sweden*, Yeats wrote to Olivia Shakespear: "I had a Swedish compliment the other day, that has pleased me better than [any] I have ever had. Some Swede said to my wife 'Our Royal Family liked your husband better than any other Nobel prize winner. They said he has the manners of a Courtier'" (Letter of August 25, 1934, *Letters*, p. 827).

55. Quoted from Anne Yeats by Marilyn Gaddis Rose, "A Visit with Anne Yeats," *Modern Drama*, 7 (December 1964), 303.

56. "A Prayer for my Daughter," *Variorum Poems*, p. 405.

57. "Estrangement," p. 300.

58. "The Bounty of Sweden," p. 337; *A Vision*, p. 279.

"I think that in early Byzantium, maybe never before or since in recorded history, religious, aesthetic and practical life were one, that architect and artificers . . . spoke to the multitude and the few alike. The painter, the mosaic worker, the worker in gold and silver, the illuminator of sacred books, were almost impersonal, almost perhaps without the consciousness of individual design, absorbed in their subject-matter and that the vision of a whole people. They could copy out of old Gospel books those pictures that seemed as sacred as the text, and yet weave all into a vast design, the work of many that seemed the work of one, that made building, picture, pattern, metal-work of rail and lamp, seem but a single image" (*A Vision*, pp. 279-280).

59. "The Bounty of Sweden," p. 337; *Variorum Poems*, p. 408.

60. *A Vision*, p. 293.

61. "Johnson's work and later Lady Gregory's work carried on the dream in a different form and it was only when Synge began to write that I saw that our movement would have to give up the deliberate creation of a kind of Holy City in the imagination, a Holy Sepulchre as it were, or Holy Grail for the Irish mind, and saw that we must be content to express the individual" (Diary entry, March 12, 1909).

62. "Estrangement," p. 301.

63. The complete text of the lecture was included at the end of the 1936 edition of *Dramatis Personae*, but dropped from *The Autobiography* published in 1938.

INDEX